Principles of Electoral Reform

Principles of
Electoral Reform

MICHAEL DUMMETT

OXFORD UNIVERSITY PRESS

*This book has been printed digitally and produced in a standard specification
in order to ensure its continuing availability*

OXFORD
UNIVERSITY PRESS

Great Clarendon Street, Oxford OX2 6DP

Oxford University Press is a department of the University of Oxford.
It furthers the University's objective of excellence in research, scholarship,
and education by publishing world-wide in

Oxford New York

Auckland Bangkok Buenos Aires Cape Town Chennai
Dar es Salaam Delhi Hong Kong Istanbul Karachi Kolkata
Kuala Lumpur Madrid Melbourne Mexico City Mumbai Nairobi
São Paulo Shanghai Taipei Tokyo Toronto

Oxford is a registered trade mark of Oxford University Press
in the UK and in certain other countries

Published in the United States
by Oxford University Press Inc., New York

ISBN 0-19-829246-5

Antony Rowe Ltd., Eastbourne

To Maurice Salles

PREFACE

ELECTORAL reform is much in the air in many countries: in Italy above all, but also in France and in Britain. In Britain, the smallest of the three national political parties has long advocated it. The British Labour Party set up the Plant Committee to report on it, and hints that, once in power, it might hold a national referendum on it; and it promises proportional representation for a Scottish Parliament. There is widespread dissatisfaction among the Italian electorate with the system that for decades produced corrupt political regimes, and uncertainty over what should replace it. And yet nowhere is there much understanding of the topic, still less sensible discussion of it. Why this paradox?

Like so much that is to be deplored, it is due to prejudice. In this case, the prejudice is to the effect that the topic is so simple that no thought or discussion is *needed*. You do not even have to stop to think whether any thought is needed: it is just *obvious* that it isn't.

Actually, to make a sensible choice of an electoral system, quite a lot of thought is needed. It is thought of which almost all those who have a vote are capable, once they have grasped the issues involved; but the issues are virtually never put to them by politicians or journalists. The issues are not put to them by those who ought to do so for two different reasons. One is that many of the politicians and journalists do not understand the issues themselves. They share the prejudice that the topic does not need thinking about; or, in the case of the politicians, they care only to advocate some system which they believe will give their respective parties the best chance in future elections. The other is that, by and large, journalists and politicians have little respect for the intelligence of ordinary voters. They do not believe that voters could understand the issues even if they were explained to them; and so even those of them who do themselves understand the issues, or partially understand them, think it best to feed the electorate with crude slogans rather than attempt serious explanation.

What do we know about the system under which Scottish electors will cast their votes when we are told that the Scottish Parliament will be elected by 'proportional representation'? We know *something*, certainly. We know that the system will have been designed to produce a Parliament whose composition by parties will roughly match the preferences, between the parties, of the electors. Is this enough to tell us what the system will be? Obviously not. Is it enough to tell us whether or not to favour that system? Perhaps this question does need a moment's thought before we see that the answer is almost equally obviously 'No.' If it needs a moment's thought, this is because we have been conditioned to think that the only question there is to be asked about an electoral system is whether or not it will yield proportional representation; it needs a moment's thought to shake off the effects of this conditioning.

The purpose of this book is to explain the issues. I am not concerned to persuade the reader to support any one electoral system that I happen to favour myself: my purpose is only to explain on what basis we should decide what electoral system we should have. The question is, surprisingly, much more complicated than one imagines before one has tried to think about it seriously. But it is well worth thinking about, because a faulty electoral system makes a mess of all our politics, and hence of a great deal of all our lives.

Michael Dummett
Oxford
December 1995

ABBREVIATIONS

AV   Alternative Vote
PR   Proportional Representation
QBS   Qualified Borda System
STV   Single Transferable Vote
WP   Winning Party (takes most)
WTA   Winner Takes All
WW   Winning (party takes most; second party takes most of the rest)

CONTENTS

CHAPTER 1

The Dual Purpose of Elections

WHAT does 'electoral reform' mean? The most common answer to this question would probably be 'the introduction of proportional representation'. And what is the problem about an electoral system? The most common answer to *this* question would probably be 'whether or not to have proportional representation'. These answers are due to conditioning—to endless repetition in newspaper articles and the speeches of politicians. If we are to think sensibly about whether we want to retain our present electoral system or switch to a different one, and, if so, which, we must begin by casting off the assumption that the *only* question to be considered is whether we are or are not in favour of PR (proportional representation). Eventually, as we shall see, we shall have to stop assuming that we know what PR is or ought to be, let alone that we know how to achieve it. But it is a beginning to grasp that whether we are for it or against it is not the only question we need to ask ourselves.

When we consider electoral reform, we frequently forget our own experiences as voters in the polling booths. What is decided by an election? By casting our votes, what do we contribute to deciding? Two different things are decided: who is to represent each individual constituency in Parliament; and what the overall composition of Parliament by political party is to be. Under a constitution such as that which obtains in Britain, in Italy, and in many other countries, the composition of Parliament decides which party shall form the Government. In some other countries, such as the United States and Russia, it does not; but in all countries it is of vital importance.

It is not the only thing of importance, however: it is also important whether those elected for the constituencies truly represent the constituencies that elected them. That is what they are in theory: representatives. And that is what they assume themselves to be: they speak in Parliament as the elected representatives of their constituencies. No doubt they should exercise their own judgement on the questions on which they have to vote, rather than conceiving themselves as mere mouthpieces for the views of the majority of their electors; but they ought to be broadly in tune with those views, and they must represent the *interests* of the locality that returned them to Parliament. It is therefore crucial to the proper functioning of a democracy that the electoral system should result in the election of genuinely representative candidates.

Many voters have felt within themselves a conflict between these two purposes of the electoral process. An elector may favour a certain political party, or even be a member of it, and yet disapprove of the candidate who is standing for that party in the (single-member) constituency in which he has a vote. The elector may dislike or distrust the candidate personally; or he may support some particular cause or policy, not that of the party as a whole, which that candidate opposes—abolition of the arms trade, say, or the legalization of marijuana. He is torn how to cast his vote: he wants his party to gain most seats in Parliament, and does not want to be disloyal to it; but his loyalty may also go to the particular cause in question, or he may simply think that it would be disastrous if that individual were elected to Parliament.

It is obviously a serious defect in an electoral system that it can place voters in such a quandary. But the dual purpose of an election produces a quandary also for anyone trying to decide on the best electoral system. Those who speak and write as though the only problem in making that decision is whether to favour PR or not presumably suppose that it does not matter who represents any given constituency. They cannot think that all electoral systems will result in the election of the same constituency representatives; if that were so, there would be no point in choosing between one electoral system and any other. But they frequently recommend a particular system on the ground that, applied across all the constituencies, it will produce a Parliament more in conformity with the proportional principle. Even if we have decided in favour of the proportional principle, however, their offering that as a compelling ground for choosing the system in question rests on a tacit assumption that has only to be stated to be seen to be false. The assumption is that it does not matter to the constituencies who is elected to represent them. But it does matter. It matters to the voters; and it matters on principle.

For anyone who realizes the importance of a sound method of selecting constituency representatives, the dual purpose of a general election poses a dilemma in hitting on the right electoral system. First, we need to determine which electoral systems will result in the election of those candidates who will most faithfully represent the electors in the constituencies. Very often, however, it is not immediately obvious, however much we know of the preferences of the electors, who those candidates are. We have therefore to frame a criterion for who would best represent the electors in a constituency, given their preferences between the candidates; having framed it, we have to pick an electoral system under which the candidates satisfying that criterion will usually win. We *also* have to frame a criterion for how Parliament ought to be divided between the political parties, given the preferences between the parties of the national electorate; having framed it, we have to pick an electoral system under which parliamentary seats will usually be so distributed. Whatever criteria we select for the two purposes, there is no reason at all that the same electoral system should usually satisfy both of them. The best to be hoped for is a clumsy compromise: a system that comes somewhere near achieving the desired result in selecting representatives for the constituencies, and somewhere near achieving the desired result in determining the composition of Parliament, but not very near either.

This is a depressing conclusion to reach at so early a stage in our enquiry. There exists a device whereby it may be avoided. The conclusion depended upon assuming what we may call the *constituency principle*. This is the principle that Parliament shall be composed exclusively of those elected to represent the constituencies. This principle is observed in both British and American elections, and, indeed, in those of almost every country in the world. If it is abandoned, however, the way is open to avoid the conclusion that the best available electoral system can be no more than a clumsy compromise. Probably many readers will already be aware of a country whose electoral system does not conform to the constituency principle—Germany. Chapter 4 will be devoted to discussing the means adopted under the German system for escaping the dilemma that has been expounded in this first chapter. Before coming to it, we shall consider how in general we should set about the problem: in what spirit we should approach the question of electoral systems. After that, we can take a preliminary look at PR and its alternatives. Then we shall turn to discuss the advantages and disadvantages of the German method of evading the constituency principle.

CHAPTER 2

How to Think about Electoral Systems

THE problem of choosing an electoral system splits into two; we saw in Chapter 1 that we have two distinct questions to answer. The first is this:

(1) Given the preferences of the electors in a constituency between the candidates, (A) which of those candidates will best represent that constituency, and (B) what system will as often as possible bring about the election of such candidates?

The second question is:

(2) Given the preferences of the electors in the nation at large between the political parties, (A) what should be the distribution of seats within Parliament among those parties, and (B) what electoral system will as often as possible bring about such a distribution?

As indicated, each of our two questions (1) and (2) is a double question and splits in turn into two. In both cases, we have first to ask (A) what it is that we want, and then (B) how we can get it. This may seem perfectly obvious; but, to judge from the manner in which electoral reform is usually discussed, it is not. Nevertheless, it holds the essential clue to how we ought to go about enquiring into the whole matter. Question (1) splits into a preliminary question, (1A), and a main question, (1B); and question (2) likewise splits into a preliminary question, (2A), and a main question, (2B). In both cases, we must address the preliminary question (A) first; if we fail to do so, our answer to the main question (B)—the question we really want to have answered—will be based on nothing but a cloudy intuitive impression, and more likely to be wrong than right, quite possibly completely wrong.

Giving our first consideration to the preliminary question (A), what we want an electoral system to do, without as yet referring to any particular such systems, is *the* key to thinking fruitfully about electoral systems. Whether we are concerning ourselves with the double question (1), the selection of constituency representatives, or with the double question (2), the composition of Parliament, the preliminary question (A) is harder than the main question (B): in general, a good deal harder. When we have answered the preliminary question (A), we shall have done the greater part of the thinking that the subject requires; armed with an answer to it, we shall usually find it comparatively easy to answer the main question (B), namely which electoral system can best be trusted to give us what we want.

Those who are disinclined to believe that any change is needed in the electoral system in force in their country may suppose that they need devote no time to any hard thinking about the subject. They are completely mistaken. Electoral reform has been a pressing issue in Italy and is becoming one in Britain, where many people passionately believe in it and advocate it; whenever the national electorate becomes gravely dissatisfied with politicians and the political process, reform of the electoral system is always likely to appeal as a remedy for the causes of that dissatisfaction. To argue that it is unnecessary and that the existing system is as satisfactory as any that could be devised requires an enquiry of exactly the same kind as does advocacy of an alternative system. In both cases it is necessary first to ask what an electoral system ought to achieve, and then to determine which system will come closest to achieving it. It makes no difference whether the eventual answer is going to be 'the system already in force' or 'such-and-such another system': in both cases, the *same* processes of thought are needed to arrive at the best answer.

Most people's image of choosing an electoral system is that of the supermarket. There are various systems on the shelves: systems in use in one country or another and systems that have been proposed but never yet adopted. We walk round the store, inspecting the systems on offer, considering them and comparing them, and make up our minds which one takes our fancy; we pick it out and go with it to the check-out counter. But this is the wrong image: the right image is DIY. Once we have done the hard work of deciding what we want an electoral system to do—once we have answered the preliminary questions (1A) and (2A)—we do not need to choose our electoral system from among those already in use or proposed. If there is not among them any that fulfils the purposes we wish to see realized, then it will usually be a comparatively simple matter to devise one ourselves.

It is almost as useless merely to give a vague answer to the preliminary question (A) 'What do we want of our electoral system?' as not to ask the question at all. If, for example, we say merely that we want it to select that one of the candidates who is the truest representative of a single-member constituency, we shall get nowhere. Given that we have decided in favour of constituencies that return only one member to Parliament, rather than two or more, the answer is indeed completely sound; but it is hazy, and therefore supplies no guidance. If, armed only with so vague an answer, we turn immediately to considering various proposed electoral systems, we shall not know how to judge them. We might reflect, for example, on the well-known two-ballot system (used in France, Russia, and elsewhere for presidential elections) under which several candidates compete in a first ballot, but, if none of them achieves an absolute majority, a run-off ballot is subsequently held which only the two candidates who gained the most votes in the first ballot are allowed to enter. Contemplating this, as used for elections in single-member constituencies, and knowing only that we want the most representative candidate to be successful, how can we tell what to say? We may have the impression that a candidate who wins under such a system is likely to be pretty representative of the constituency electorate as a whole: but how can we test this impression, and what arguments can we bring in its favour? How can we be sure that the winner under this system will always be more representative than any of the candidates who came third or lower on the first ballot?

Whether we are concerned with question (1), the selection of constituency representatives, or with question (2), the composition of Parliament, our question is twofold: (A) what do we want? and (B) how can we get it? We cannot tackle (B) successfully until we have answered (A) *precisely*. We must, for example, decide more than that the successful candidate must truly represent the constituency electorate: we must decide exactly which candidate, characterized in terms of the voters' preferences, is to count as the most representative. Only if we have first decided this are we in a position to judge whether a given electoral system is, from this standpoint, a good one or not. Without having decided it, we are choosing between electoral systems *blindly*.

The key to deciding on the electoral system we want is thus to address ourselves first of all to the preliminary questions (1A) and (2A). Let us for the present use (1A) as our example, as applied to single-member constituencies. We have to find a precise answer to the question which one, of a given set of candidates in some constituency, will most truly represent the electors of that constituency. On what basis should it be judged which is the most representative candidate? Only facts of one kind are relevant: the preferences of the electors as between the candidates.

Some may be tempted to give a more restricted answer, namely that all that matters is which candidate each elector prefers to all the others—which candidate is each elector's first choice. Those inclined to say this are probably influenced solely by the electoral system with which they are most familiar, such as that at present in force in Britain and generally known there as 'First Past the Post': under this, a voter has an opportunity to do no more than make a cross against the name of only one candidate, the candidate obtaining the greatest number of such votes being elected. The claim that is sometimes made, that all that matters is which candidate is each elector's first choice, illustrates once more how differently people think when they are theorizing about electoral systems and when they are themselves actually voting. For, when people are actually voting, even under the so-called 'First Past the Post' system, they do *not* always behave as though all they cared about was whether or not the candidate each of them most favours will be successful. If they did, then, having decided on their single preferred candidate, they would never be in any dilemma on how to cast their votes under that system; but they often are. They are, because in actual fact they mind greatly who wins, even if the candidate of their first choice does not. Some voters, believing that their favoured candidate has little or no chance of winning, will vote for some other candidate they think the best of those they consider to have a serious chance. Other voters, caring more that a certain candidate should be defeated than that the one they most favour should win, may vote for whoever they judge is the most likely to defeat the candidate they detest.

In any such case, people are moved to cast their votes as they do by preferences that they have between candidates neither of whom is their first choice. Any preference between candidates that may determine how an elector decides to vote must be relevant to which candidate would best represent the electorate; and there is no saying which of an elector's preferences might not influence his decision how to cast his vote. The 'First Past the Post' system does not give the voters the opportunity to express all their preferences between the candidates, and hence all the preferences that would be relevant to determining what the outcome ought to be under a just system. That is a grave defect indeed. First, it inevitably creates a quandary for some of the voters, who are unsure by which of their preferences to be guided when they cast their votes. And secondly, it cannot fail to fall short of delivering the ideal outcome. Suppose that we have devised an exact criterion, based on the voters' preferences, for the most representative candidate. Then no electoral system that does not allow the voters to express all those preferences can possibly be relied on to result in the election of the candidate who satisfies that criterion, since there will be no sure way of telling, from the votes, which candidate that is.

Our criterion for the most representative candidate must be based on the electors' *actual* preferences. These, however, will never be revealed for certain by how they fill in their ballot papers. One reason for this holds good only under some electoral systems, the other under all of them. Under 'First Past the Post' and many other systems, the voters are given no opportunity to express all their preferences. Several other systems give them such an opportunity, by requiring or allowing them to list all the candidates in order of preference. When any such system is used, it will be possible to gain an approximate indication of voters' preferences between all the candidates from the ballot papers they return. Even in this case, however, the indication will not be exact, or, if it is, we cannot know that it is, because of the possibility of tactical voting. Under all electoral systems, some voters may vote tactically, that is to say, in a way that does not conform to their true preferences. It can be mathematically demonstrated that no system can avoid this. That is to say, there can be no system under which, given his preferences, every voter will always have only one way of voting that will bring about an outcome as desirable as possible from his point of view, however the others choose to cast their votes. Nevertheless, different systems vary greatly in the degree of incentive they give for tactical voting. A system that debars a voter even from expressing all his preferences (or takes minimal account of most of them) gives the most potent of all incentives for it. That is why tactical voting plays so large a role in elections under the 'First Past the Post' system.

What is the point of basing a criterion for the most truly representative of the candidates upon the voters' actual preferences between them, if we cannot ever tell for sure, after the election, what these were? Or, equally, of basing a principle for how parliamentary seats should be distributed among the parties upon the voters' actual preferences between *them*, if, again, we cannot tell for sure what *those* preferences were? Obviously, it cannot be in order to judge, after a particular general election or constituency election, whether the electoral system under which it was conducted delivered the desirable outcome. It is, rather, to assess *in advance* the probability that a given system will deliver the desirable outcome—will do what we want an electoral system to do. We can assess this by constructing hypothetical distributions of preferences among a set of voters, and then examining what the outcome will be under a given system if they all vote sincerely, and what incentives the system offers them for voting tactically. This is the principal, indeed the only practicable, technique for investigating the merits of rival electoral systems.

Is tactical voting to be deplored? Certainly not because it is dishonest or undemocratic. A ballot paper instructs the voter to place a cross or a numeral against the name of one or more candidates: it does not ask the voter to reveal his true opinions by doing so, and, if it did, that would be an impertinence rightly ignored. A voting mechanism, such as that incorporated in an electoral system, is a device for aggregating the diverse wishes of a number of people; each voter, knowing how the result will be determined from the votes cast, is entitled to use it in whatever way he thinks most likely to bring about a result more acceptable to him than that which would be produced by his voting differently. The labelling of one way of voting as 'sincere' and another as 'tactical' depends upon somewhat arbitrarily interpreting the ballot paper as asking the voter a question, for instance 'Which of the candidates would you most like to see elected?' If we were to interpret it as asking a slightly different question, for instance, 'Which, among those candidates whom you believe to have a genuine chance, would you most like to see elected?', we should turn a 'tactical' vote into a 'sincere' one. But the truth is that the ballot-paper does not ask the voter a question at all, unless it be 'Which way of casting your vote do you think most likely to bring about a result acceptable to you?'. And that, unless he has been intimidated or bribed, he cannot but answer sincerely.

Nor is tactical voting to be deprecated on the ground that it will tend to bring about an unfair result. If an electoral system is in force that will usually bring about the fairest possible result when everyone votes sincerely, then indeed tactical voting, when effective, will obviously in general produce a less fair result; for, if it was effective, it must have produced a different result from that which would have followed if all had voted sincerely, and that, by hypothesis, would probably have been the fairest possible. But when the electoral system in force often brings about an unfair result when everyone votes sincerely, tactical voting will often compensate for its defects. Suppose that Miss Morris is voting between three candidates, A, B, and C, under a system that instructs her to place a cross against the name of just one of them. She believes that A is decidedly the best candidate, but strongly prefers B to C. Holding the well-informed view that A has little chance of being elected, she may give her vote to B. Mr Jenkins, with the same set of preferences, may feel that the most important thing is to prevent C from getting into Parliament, and may likewise vote for B, rightly believing B to have a greater chance of defeating C than A does. Both have used their votes to express their preferences for the candidate of their second choice over the one they liked least; and it may well be that, if others of like mind did the same, the result will be fairer than if every voter had voted 'sincerely', that is, for the candidate of his first choice.

Tactical voting *is* to be deprecated, all the same. This is because, to be successful, the tactical voter must have good information, or make an accurate guess, about how everyone else is likely to vote. If he is well informed about this, and if other voters who share his opinions are equally well informed and adopt the same tactics, he and they will probably achieve their objective. But if a voter essays a tactical vote on the basis of a misapprehension about what other voters are likely to do, he, and others who make the same mistake, are likely to bring about a result that they like less well than the one that would have been produced if they had voted sincerely. When the electoral system in force is a poor one, opinion polls will therefore help the voters to judge how best to vote, and by this means contribute to bringing about fairer results than would have been achieved otherwise; there is then no ground for forbidding them near to the election. Yet opinion polls are notoriously unreliable, and often less reliable than individual judgement. It is no part of democracy to reward those well informed about other voters' intentions and to penalize those ill informed about them; the wishes and opinions of the latter are of equal significance with those of the former. It is for this reason that tactical voting ought to be discouraged.

It can in part be discouraged, not by exhortation, but by restricting information. We have seen that, when a sound electoral system is in operation, tactical voting will tend to produce less fair results. In such a case, then, the less opportunity voters have to estimate the voting intentions of others, the less tactical voting there will be; there will then be a ground for prohibiting opinion polls well in advance of an election. But the most effective means of discouraging tactical voting is to adopt an electoral system that offers few incentives for it.

How, then, ought we to set about choosing or devising an electoral system? Let us for the moment pretend that we are not concerned with the overall composition of Parliament (question 2), but only with the selection of the most representative candidates for the constituencies (question 1); and pretend further that we have agreed to have only single-member constituencies. We have first to frame a criterion for the most representative candidate, given the preferences of the voters (preliminary question 1A). To repeat: this is the *essential* first step; without it, there can be no method for determining which electoral system to adopt. Having solved this problem, we should seek an electoral system which will usually bring about the election of the candidate satisfying that criterion whenever all the votes are sincere. We have then to scrutinize this system to make sure that it will not offer too great an incentive for tactical voting; if it does, we must modify it, even at the sacrifice of some effectiveness in guaranteeing the most desirable result under sincere voting.

This is not a recipe for finding a perfect electoral system: there is no perfect system. It is a recipe for finding the best that can be found; no better recipe is possible. Contemplating various possible systems without having thought out what we want them to achieve, and making hazy guesses about their political effects, is no recipe at all.

CHAPTER 3

PR and the
Alternative to it

THE second of our two questions was this:

Given the preferences of the electors in the nation at large between the political parties, (A) what should be the distribution of seats within Parliament among those parties, and (B) what electoral system will as often as possible bring about such a distribution?

This chapter is devoted to a first look at the first half of this second double question, that is, to question (2A). We shall not be concerned with what electoral system will achieve whatever result we decide that we want; only with what the division of parliamentary seats between the parties ought to be, given the preferences of the electorate.

Many people—perhaps even most people—suppose this to be the *only* problem that anyone needs to think about in order to decide whether his country already has the best possible electoral system or whether it needs to be changed. As was observed in Chapter 1, they are greatly mistaken: the question whether the system in force selects MPs who are truly representative of their constituencies is equally problematic, and significantly harder to resolve. They are right to this extent, however, that electors care more about the composition of Parliament, and that it and, in countries such as Britain, the consequent colour of the government, make a greater difference to their lives than the identity of their constituency MPs. In any case, since many people apparently regard the problem of securing MPs truly representative of their constituencies as negligible, but nurture a deep interest in the composition of Parliament by parties, it is worth taking a preliminary look at the latter problem at this stage; we shall return to it later.

The constitutions of most countries provide for a division of the legislature into a lower and an upper chamber, with somewhat different powers and elected under different systems: in Britain at present (1996) the upper House is not elected at all. If there is a ground for electing the two chambers by different methods, this must lie in the difference between the roles that they are intended to play, and this difference varies greatly from one national constitution to another. In this book, therefore, we shall not enquire into different modes of electing the lower and the upper House, but simply consider the composition of Parliament generally. The case for dividing the parliamentary representation of the political parties in proportion to their electoral support must, when there are two chambers, apply to both of them; likewise, the case against doing so must apply to both, though doubtless more strongly to the lower House if it is its political composition that decides who forms the government.

The rationale of PR is obvious. The principle is that seats in Parliament should be allotted to the political parties in the same proportion—or as near to it as is feasible—as support for those parties is divided among the national electorate. Here an elector is deemed to support a given party if it is his first choice among the parties; under a system that observes the constituency principle, so that electors' votes are cast solely for individual candidates standing in their constituencies, an elector is regarded as supporting that party to which the candidate of his first choice (understood as being the one for whom he voted) belonged. Thus, if there are 650 Parliamentary seats, a party that has 10 per cent support among the electorate will be allotted 65 of them. Even this may create minor problems. If, as in the present British Parliament, there are 651 seats, it is obvious that we should then normally round down, and still allot only 65 seats to such a party. But suppose that there were 655 seats: should we round down to 65 or up to 66? Or suppose that there were five parties, obtaining respectively 35.4 per cent, 29.4 per cent, 22.4 per cent, 7.4 per cent, and 5.4 per cent support. If there were 600 parliamentary seats, the corresponding shares would be 212.4, 176.4, 134.4, 44.4, and 32.4. If we rounded down in each case, we should leave two seats unfilled: to which parties should those two seats go? This is a tricky problem, which has been studied in detail, for this and other contexts. But it is a minor problem, which we may here leave aside.

PR is often applied with a *threshold*. If a party has failed to obtain a certain minimum percentage of support—often fixed at 5 per cent—it will get *no* representation in Parliament, at least unless it has succeeded in getting one or more of its candidates elected to represent constituencies; Parliamentary seats are then divided among the other political parties in the same proportion as their national support. The principal purpose of the threshold is to deny representation to extremist parties.

The rationale of PR is, plainly, that each parliamentary seat should represent approximately the same proportion of the national electorate. This, the advocates of PR maintain, is the only fair principle to follow in what proclaims itself to be a representative democracy. It is unjust when six times as many votes are needed to elect each MP of one party as are needed for each MP of another: in such a case, supporters of the first party are indisputably under-represented, and those of the second correspondingly over-represented.

Opponents of PR obviously support some principle of *dis*proportional representation. They never express their opinion in this way. What they usually say is that they believe in effective government—or in firm, strong, or stable government. This, however, is to characterize a principle for the distribution of seats in Parliament by the effect that its supporters claim for it. That effect may be disputed. Still more may it be disputed that the effect can be obtained only by distributing seats between the parties in the way favoured by opponents of PR: supporters of PR are entitled to contest the implication that their principle will result in ineffective, flimsy, weak, or unstable government. It is better to use a name for the principle which opponents of PR believe ought to govern the distribution of parliamentary seats that describes, not the effects that are tendentiously claimed for it, but how it operates.

Any method of distributing parliamentary seats between the parties that diverges from the proportional principle might be called 'disproportional representation', which is therefore a quite imprecise term. A great many of those who oppose PR do so because they regard with horror what is called in Britain a 'hung Parliament', that is, one in which no party commands a majority. The fundamental principle to which they adhere is that whichever party secures the highest proportion of support among the electorate as a whole ought to be allotted an absolute majority of seats in Parliament; this might be called the 'Winner Take All' principle (WTA) (more precise would be 'Winner Take Most'). We need not stop to consider exactly how the size of the winning party's parliamentary majority should be calculated. The proportion of votes for the most successful party out of the total votes cast would have to be multiplied by a suitable factor to arrive at the proportion of parliamentary seats awarded to it. What this factor must be to guarantee that it will have a parliamentary majority depends on how many parties there are. If there are only three parties, the most successful of them will necessarily secure more than a third of the total votes; it will therefore be sufficient to multiply the proportion of the total electoral vote it obtains by $\frac{3}{2}$ to arrive at the proportion of the parliamentary seats it is to have. If there were four parties, the most successful might conceivably obtain only just over a quarter of the total vote, in which case the multiplier would have to be set at 2. But, plainly, the multiplier would have to taper off as the proportion of the total vote obtained by the most successful party increased, for it would be outrageous if, with four parties, one triumphantly securing 50 per cent of the total vote were to be allotted 100 per cent of the parliamentary seats; perhaps, whatever the number of parties, the multiplier could be set at 1.1 for a party obtaining half the votes of the electorate. In devising a formula for the multiplier, there would be no need for the number of parties to enter into it: it could simply guarantee that a party gaining any given proportion of the total votes would have a majority in Parliament, provided that it was the highest proportion gained by any party.

This tells us only what proportion of parliamentary seats ought, according to WTA, to go to the most successful party. WTA is a nugatory principle if, as in the United States, there are normally only two political parties; for then, unless the geographical distribution of support for the parties is exceedingly irregular, the most successful party is certain to have an absolute majority of the total vote, and virtually certain to have a majority in Parliament (or equivalent representative assembly). The WTA principle therefore needs to be supplemented by a rule to determine the proportion of parliamentary seats to be allotted to the other parties. The reason why British opponents of PR are never explicit on the point is that they see no need to do anything but *oppose* change. The 'First Past the Post' system that now prevails in Britain does not *always* preclude a hung Parliament. Moreover, it cannot be trusted to allot a greater number of parliamentary seats to a party with a higher proportion of the national vote. In the British general election of 1951, the Conservatives won 321 seats in the House of Commons with 48.0 per cent of the national vote, against 295 seats for Labour with 48.8 per cent of the national vote; in that of February 1974, the Labour party had 37.1 per cent of the national vote, and 301 seats in Parliament, while the Conservatives, with 37.9 per cent of the national vote, obtained only 297 seats. To this extent, therefore, the system is, for proponents of WTA, an imperfect one. But it usually assigns to the most successful party a substantial majority in Parliament, and it is that which WTA supporters care most about. They are terrified that, if the very possibility of a change in the electoral system is once conceded, they would end up with some variety of PR. Since the existing system is in general satisfactory to them, and only occasionally produces a result counter to their wishes, they deem their best strategy to consist in keeping rather quiet about what exactly they want, and resolutely opposing change of any kind. Best let sleeping dogs lie, however restless their sleep may be.

Advocates of WTA have two options when the distribution of parliamentary seats to parties other than the most successful one is in contention. Some may argue that, for government to be as effective as possible, the opposition should be as ineffective as possible, which will happen when it is as divided as possible. They will therefore support the distribution of the seats not allotted to the most successful party to the other parties in proportion to their relative support among the electorate. We might adopt the label 'WP' for this version of WTA (the winning party takes most, and the remaining seats are divided proportionally among the others). Suppose that there are three parties, Blue, Red, and Yellow, which obtain 40 per cent, 35 per cent and 25 per cent of the national vote respectively. Suppose, further, that the Blue Party is allotted 52 per cent of the seats in Parliament, corresponding to a multiplier of 1.3; such an outcome would be moderate in an election held under the British system ('First Past the Post' with the constituency principle). There remain 48 per cent of the seats to be allotted to the Red and Yellow Parties. Under WP, 28 per cent of the total seats would go to the Red Party, and 20 per cent to the Yellow Party, corresponding exactly to their 35:25 shares of the national vote. The Red Party, with 35 per cent of the national vote, would have obtained little more than half as many parliamentary seats as the Blue Party, with 40 per cent.

Alternatively, it might be held that, for a healthy democracy, as effective an opposition is needed as is consistent with a parliamentary majority for the party that (under the British system) is to form the government. This necessity may then be taken to entail that a disproportionate number of the seats not allotted to the government party shall go to the second most successful party, leaving only a negligible number for any remaining parties. This is, of course, the usual effect of the British electoral system. Such a version of WTA may be labelled 'WW' (the winning party takes most of the seats, and the second most successful party takes most of the rest). Thus, in the foregoing example, of the 48 per cent of parliamentary seats available for the two opposition parties, 36 per cent of the total might, under WW, go to the Red Party and only 12 per cent to the Yellow Party, which thus, with more than half as many national votes as the Blue Party, will obtain less than a quarter of its representation in Parliament. Opponents of PR must think out which of the two versions of WTA they take to be the sounder. They will not have to ask which is fairer or gives better representation to the electorate: both versions rest solidly on political considerations, not on those of fairness or of representing the electorate.

For supporters of WTA, fair representation of the

electors is of less importance than effective government. For them, effective government is possible only if no party has to share power with any other, and the party in power is able to push through whatever legislation it wishes without effective obstruction. For supporters of PR, on the other hand, this is temporary dictatorship. When the opinion of the electorate is divided, they argue, it is best served, not by a government committed to a set of policies of which only a minority of the electorate approves, but by one in which more than one party participates, and which therefore has to pursue policies arrived at by compromise. Moreover, a system which seldom gives a parliamentary majority to a single party will secure a large measure of continuity in government policy, in place of successive lurches from one radical policy to another, each carried out against the wishes of a majority of the public. Such a more continuous policy will be able to make gradual adjustments in response to alterations in public opinion, perhaps by means of shifts in the ruling coalition. Continuity and responsiveness, advocates of PR argue, are of greater value than unimpeded power.

We are all in favour of effective government in the same sense as that in which we are all in favour of peace and prosperity. That is why it is impertinent of opponents of PR to arrogate the phrase 'effective government' as the label for the principle they support. It is especially impertinent when supporters of PR are able to point to political benefits arguably as great as those of WTA. Opponents of PR would be uneasy if the question asked in a referendum were 'Do you support proportional or disproportional representation?'; but a swindle would be perpetrated upon the public if the question were 'Do you support proportional representation or effective government?'. The dispute between PR and WTA does not lie, however, within the competence of electoral theory as such. It is, rather, a straightforwardly political question, about which, therefore, readers must at this point be left to make up their minds.

In this chapter we have considered only that objection to PR that is most commonly brought against it. In Chapter 13 we shall concern ourselves with a quite different objection to PR as ordinarily understood.

CHAPTER 4

The Dual-Vote Device

UNDER the existing German electoral system, each voter casts two votes in a general election. The first is a vote between the candidates for his constituency, and goes to determine which of them is to represent the constituency in the Bundestag (the equivalent of the House of Commons). The second is a vote between the political parties contesting the election in the voter's *Land* (region), and goes to determine the composition of the Bundestag by parties.

As it is used in the German system, this dual-vote device is in the service of proportional representation (with a threshold). The constituency elections are held under the system used in Britain: each elector votes for a single candidate, and the candidate obtaining the greatest number of votes is elected and becomes a member of the Bundestag. The elector likewise casts his second vote for a single one of the parties. Each party is then allotted seats in the Bundestag in accordance with the ratio of votes it obtained nationally, with a threshold of 5 per cent of the national vote or three constituency seats; parties that have not achieved the threshold are allowed to keep any constituency seats they have won. For this to work, there have to be other members of the Bundestag in addition to those elected to represent the constituencies, in order to make up the representation of the various parties to the correct proportions; in fact, there are just as many additional members as constituency representatives. The seats allocated to each party are distributed among the regions (*Länder*) in proportion to the votes obtained by that party in each region; the additional members are selected from a list provided by the party in that region. The German electoral system is thus an amalgam of three different components: the dual vote device; the so-called 'First Past the Post' system for constituency elections; and proportional representation for determining the representation of parties in the Bundestag. We do not need any discussion of this system as a whole: each of its three components will be looked at separately. In this chapter we shall be concerned with the dual-vote device.

In this way, the constituency principle, according to which Parliament (more exactly, its lower House) should be composed exclusively of those elected to represent the constituencies, is violated. It is, obviously, essential to flout the constituency principle if the dual vote is to be effective: the provision for additional members is an integral part of the dual-vote device. The converse is not true: the Hansard Society has proposed an adaptation of the German system under which each elector casts only a single vote, namely for one of those standing for his constituency. The additional members would then be allocated among the parties by treating a vote for a candidate of any given party as a vote for that party. This modification would retain the essence of the German system, in that it would separate the principle determining the composition of Parliament from that by which constituencies choose their representatives. But it hardly seems an improvement on the German system: it would deprive the voters of the freedom to vote for a party different from that of the individual candidate, thus restoring the dilemma faced under any system according with the constituency principle by voters who would like to split their votes in this way if they could.

It is important to observe that the dual-vote device is, in itself, entirely independent of the method adopted to elect constituency representatives, and equally independent of the principle adopted for determining the composition of Parliament. Provided that the voters are allowed to do more than simply nominate a single candidate, for example, to rank the candidates in order of preference, it can be combined with any mechanism that may be favoured for choosing the representative of a constituency on the basis of the returned ballot papers (or, equally, for choosing the several representatives of a multi-member constituency). Likewise, the dual-vote device could be used with any preferred method for determining how Parliament shall be divided between the parties. It is usually thought of as a version of proportional representation, because it is so used in Germany. It could, however, just as well be used in the service of the 'Winner Take All' form of disproportional representation, explained in the last chapter: additional members would then be supplied by the party having the greatest number of votes cast in its favour, in order to ensure that it commanded an absolute majority in Parliament. The dual-vote device, as such, is completely neutral both about the selection of representatives and about the composition of Parliament: it is simply a device for separating the two purposes of a general election. The number of additional members would not need to amount to half the total number of MPs, as under the German system; the Hansard Society proposes that it be only a quarter, and this would usually be enough for whatever purpose—proportional or disproportional—was aimed at.

A quite valid objection is brought against all systems involving party lists, that they give too much power to the political parties. We are so used to political parties that we tend to think of them as integral to the functioning of a democratic system; some of their members feel towards them a loyalty more appropriate to a religious body. Yet in fact their very existence infringes the ideal of democracy. They are in essence conspiracies in accordance with which their parliamentary representatives agree to vote in unison in order to make more votes go as their individual members wish than would happen if everyone voted according to his true opinion. In the British House of Commons, this function of the political parties is highly institutionalized by the system of whips and the practice of expelling from their party MPs who defy them.

It is obvious that the outcome of a vote is more likely to be the expression of the general will if all who participate in it vote according to their true opinions than if some, in collusion with others, vote contrary to those opinions. Such collusion may nevertheless be advantageous to the voters who engage in it: that is a large part of the purpose of political parties. Suppose that three motions are voted on in succession in a legislature with 600 members, of whom not one favours all three motions. 120 of them favour the first two motions, but not the third, the same number favour the first and the third, but not the second, and the same number again favour the second and the third, but not the first; the remaining 240 members are opposed to all three motions. Then, if all the members vote according to their true opinions, all three motions will be defeated by 360 votes to 240. If, however, the 360 members each of whom favours two of the three motions collude to vote for each of the motions, they will all be carried by 360 votes to 240. Each of those 360 members will have achieved the result he favoured on two out of three of the motions, whereas, if they had voted sincerely, they would each have achieved the result they favoured on only one of the three. To the extent that the members' true opinions were a sound guide to what would have been for the best, or to what the electorate desired, the collusion converted the best possible outcome into the worst possible outcome; but those who engaged in it could congratulate themselves on a skilful piece of political manipulation. That, in miniature, is the purpose of political parties.

Nevertheless, the existence of political parties is probably an inescapable evil. It is usually in dictatorships that all political parties, or all but one, are proscribed; a one-party state is of course a form of dictatorship. Uganda is currently experimenting with a no-party state—a democratic system under which the formation of political parties is not allowed; there is naturally an accusation that this gives excessive power to the incumbent régime, and it remains to be seen whether such a system can be worked without degenerating into a dictatorship. In normal democracies in which political parties function, they play a larger role in the electoral process than is by anyone else's standard desirable, since they select the candidates between whom the voters have to choose. Moreover, the power of a political party to dictate, influence, or interfere with the selection of candidates for Parliament is the more inimical to democracy the more centralized it is. If it is in the hands of a regional office, or, still worse, of the central office of the party, a rigid conformity to the current party line will result. A local constituency selection committee may continue over the years to nominate a deviant adherent to the party, such as Sir Winston Churchill, who disagrees fundamentally with its prevailing policy, but who would never be tolerated by the central office if it could help doing so.

For this reason, the use of party lists to supply the additional MPs called for by an electoral system using the dual-vote device is unarguably a serious defect in such a system. It may be mitigated by selecting the additional MPs from those unsuccessful candidates in the constituency elections who achieved the best results by percentage of votes cast. If, as under the German system, the additional members are allocated by region, these would be drawn from those who stood for constituencies within the region. Alternatively, the electors voting for a given party could be given an opportunity to vote for particular candidates on the party's list, those appointed as additional members being those who obtained the greatest number of votes (as is done in the list system in use in Finland). This would complicate the process of voting, however, and would be workable only if none of those who stood as candidates for constituencies were allowed to be included on their party's list, a prohibition that would be a serious drawback. However this flaw in the German system is corrected, the dual-vote device has a decisive advantage over systems conforming to the constituency principle.

This advantage lies in its separating the two purposes of a general election from one another, giving each elector a separate vote for each purpose. The advantage is great for an elector whose wish for a certain party to have the greatest success in the general election conflicts with his preferences among the candidates standing in his constituency: when the dual-vote device is used, he is no longer in any quandary.

For anyone engaged in thinking about electoral systems, the advantage is more than great: it is overwhelming. It is the purpose of this book to encourage its readers to think about this subject; and the mere existence of the dual-vote device liberates us from having to try to find or devise an electoral system that will carry out the two distinct purposes of an election in the best manner possible. We can, instead, think about each separately. We can decide on the best voting mechanism for electing representatives of the constituencies without regard to its effect on the composition of Parliament. And we can likewise decide how we should like parliamentary seats to be allocated to the parties, given the preferences of the electorate between them, without regard to how they will be allotted by whatever method of electing constituency representatives we decide in favour of. We can do this, because we know that we need not abide by the constituency principle. If the method of electing constituency representatives that we decide upon would, if the constituency principle were followed, yield a Parliament divided among the parties in a manner we consider inappropriate, this can be corrected by allowing electors a second vote as between the parties, and appointing additional MPs in accordance with the results of this second vote in order to adjust the imbalance.

We do not need, before we proceed further with our study of electoral systems, to decide in advance to propose adoption of the dual vote. If we are lucky enough to hit on a method of electing constituency representatives that will result in a Parliament suitably divided between the parties, without the need for additional members, then we may dispense with the dual vote. This will still have the disadvantage of leaving some electors in a quandary over how to cast their votes so as to satisfy their wishes both for the overall national result and for the result in their local constituencies; but that may be thought to be a price worth paying for avoiding the trouble of dual votes and a procedure for appointing additional MPs that will hardly be needed. The importance of the dual-vote device consists in the fact that it *could* be adopted if called for, not that it *must* be incorporated into any satisfactory electoral system. It is the fact that it *could* be resorted to that liberates us, in our capacity as theorists, from the necessity of keeping quite a different objective in mind while thinking about another, and of having recourse to any uneasy compromise between the two objectives, when we have settled what they should be.

CHAPTER 5

Who will Win? Who ought to Win?

VOTING is used to resolve differences of *opinion* and differences of *desire*, usually a mixture of the two. Suppose that an appointments committee, having interviewed the applicants for a post of librarian and studied their testimonials, has drawn up a short list of six: the committee members now proceed to a vote. They are probably all agreed on the qualities needed in a librarian, but differ only on which of the applicants has them to the highest degree: this is therefore a pure case of voting to resolve differences of opinion. The aim of the voting procedure is to select that applicant who, on the basis of the committee members' judgements, most probably possesses the desired qualities. If an outsider, to whom neither the applicants nor the committee members were known personally, were told the voters' rankings of those on the short list, he could, in the light of those rankings, form a judgement about which applicant was the most likely to be the best: it is that applicant whom the voting procedure ought to select as the one to be appointed.

In such a case, it is the aim of the voting procedure to be

fair to the *candidates*; it is no part of its purpose to be fair to the *voters*. If the committee has had to make three appointments to different posts, none of its members has any right to complain that his opinion has been passed over every time: the point of voting was to choose the best candidates, not to give satisfaction to the committee members. A case at the opposite extreme would be that of club members voting to decide how to spend a sum of money that had unexpectedly accrued to the club funds. Here they are probably all quite aware of the consequences of spending it in any one of the various ways that have been proposed: they disagree only on what they *want*. In such a case, the purpose of voting is to arrive at a resultant of divergent wishes; the aim is to be fair to the voters. Unlike the preceding case, therefore, the voting procedure ought therefore to be one that favours compromise, by arriving at a decision that will give some pleasure to as many as possible of the members, even if certain of them would have derived greater pleasure from other decisions.

Elections, to Parliament or to a local council, resemble the second type more than the first. They have, however, a special purpose, to choose *representatives*: people who can speak in the name of the residents of the constituency or ward, who know what they want or need and can voice those wants and needs. It is in the light of that purpose that we must judge the merits of an electoral system.

We have two questions to answer: (1) what system to use for electing representatives of a constituency; and (2) how to achieve the best distribution of parliamentary seats among the political parties. In both cases, we must *first* decide what we should aim at: which candidates will most truly represent their constituencies; and what is the desirable division of seats in Parliament among the parties. Only when we have delineated our objectives in specific terms should we consider how to attain them. Question (1) bifurcates, however. Under the present British electoral system, each constituency returns just one member to Parliament, although it has not always been so. Under any reasonable method of election, a large constituency returning three, four or five members to Parliament will be better at selecting representatives than a small one returning only one, because it will nearly always accord success to candidates supported by different sections of the electorate; this is why multi-member constituencies are usually favoured by enthusiasts for PR. We have therefore to consider question (1) separately for single- and for multi-member constituencies. It is best to answer the question for each of them separately before deciding which of them we favour: we can then decide this in the light of our answer to question (2). If our favoured method of election in single-member constituencies proves likely to yield a better distribution of parliamentary seats than our favoured method of election in multi-member ones, we shall presumably prefer to have single-member constituencies; conversely if it is the other way round.

Since the problem of choosing an electoral system for multi-member constituencies is more complicated than that of choosing one for single-member constituencies, we shall do best to begin by considering the latter: it will be to that problem that the rest of this chapter, together with Chapters 6 to 9, will be devoted. Chapters 10 to 12 will be concerned with elections in multi-member constituencies. We have already taken a brief look at question (2) in Chapters 3 and 4; we shall revert to it in Chapter 13.

When there are only two candidates standing for election, there is of course no problem about how the choice between them is to be made: each elector must be asked to vote for one of them, and the one obtaining a majority declared elected. In the United States, there are only two parties that have shown themselves capable of enduring, although third parties come into temporary existence from time to time. Even in presidential elections, when the whole country forms in effect one vast constituency, there are usually only two significant candidates. The problem whether the electoral system demands reform is for this reason much less acute in the United States; this is not to say that it cannot be raised at all. For it still has to be asked whether a more representative Congress would not result from the use of multi-member constituencies; moreover, there are sometimes more than two serious candidates offering themselves, even in presidential elections. The question whether the system of electing a president needs or is capable of reform is of course complicated by the fact that the country is after all a federation, and by the anachronistic exigencies of the Constitution.

The term 'First Past the Post', which has gained almost universal acceptance for the system currently in use in both Britain and the United States, illustrates how little thought is commonly given to electoral systems; for the name is blatantly inappropriate. There is no post: no proportion of votes that a candidate has to attain to be elected. If an election is to be compared to a race, then the name 'First Past the Post' should be given to one in which, in the course of repeated ballots, that candidate is declared the winner who first achieves, say, 50 per cent of the total votes cast. An election held under the British and American system usually miscalled by that name should be compared, rather, to a race in which the winner is the competitor who, after a fixed length of time, is ahead of the others. The system is best called the *plurality* system, since it demands that the winner obtain, not a majority of the votes, but merely *more* of them than any of the other candidates. We may start our enquiry by contemplating a hypothetical election under the plurality system.

Suppose that an election is held in a constituency under the plurality system. There are three candidates, **A**, **B**, and **C**: the results are declared as follows:

> **B**: 23,678
> **C**: 23,040
> **A**: 9,417

B has won by a narrow majority.

Was this a fair result? Is **B** the most representative of the three candidates? We cannot tell: we do not know if any of the electors voted tactically.

Suppose that we come to learn that, if every voter had voted sincerely, that is, for the candidate of his first choice, the results would have been:

> **B**: 19,668
> **C**: 22,033
> **A**: 14,434

C would in this case have won. There has obviously been tactical voting on the part of **A**'s supporters.

Some, out of disapproval of tactical voting, may say that the actual outcome was unfair: if everyone had voted sincerely, C would have won. But this is to miss the point. We are not trying to judge whether the result was fair in the light of the electoral system; we are trying to judge the electoral system in the light of the result. We could, from the data to hand, judge that the result was unfair, and hence the electoral system which led to it a bad one, only if we believed that the one true criterion for whether a candidate would best represent his constituency is the number of voters whose first choice he is. It seems impossible to devise a system that will ascertain to whom this criterion applies. The natural method of doing so is by means of the plurality system. This, however, offers strong incentives for tactical voting, as in the hypothetical case under consideration. Advocates of the criterion will therefore condemn it for doing so: but what other system can do better in this regard?

How, if we do not adopt this criterion, are we to decide whether the result imagined was fair or unfair? It surely depends on whether or not a majority of the electors would have preferred C to have been elected. This, however, we cannot tell from the information so far given. A's 9,417 supporters who remained loyal to him had no means of indicating which of the other two candidates they preferred. If 5,028 of them or more preferred C to B, then a majority of the entire electorate preferred C to B, and B's victory was therefore unfair. But if 4,390 or more of them preferred B to C, then a majority of the entire electorate preferred B to C, and B's victory constituted the election of the most representative candidate.

Those supporters of A who voted tactically obviously

decided that the candidate of their first choice did not have a real chance, or at least not enough of a chance to make their voting for him worth while. Were they right? We may suppose that none of the supporters of C, knowing that he had a very strong chance, would have deserted him: he was therefore assured of 22,033 votes. The maximum number of votes that A could have obtained would be the number of his supporters (14,434) plus the number of supporters of B who preferred A to C (supposing, as is very unlikely, that they were all to vote tactically for A). If there were fewer than 7,600 of the latter, A would have been unable to defeat C in even the most favourable circumstances.

This, then, provides a clear criterion for a candidate's having no chance whatever under the plurality system. It is that, compared with whichever rival candidate has the largest body of supporters whose first choice he is, the number of voters preferring the given candidate to that rival one should be less than the number of the rival candidate's supporters. It may well be so in our example: the number of voters preferring A to C may be less than the number whose first choice is C. If so, those of A's supporters who concluded that he had no chance and voted tactically in consequence were objectively right to do so, if we set aside the value of demonstrating support for him and his party; but it was difficult for them to be sure that they were right.

It quite frequently happens, under the plurality system, that numerous supporters of the least popular of three leading candidates realize—or mistakenly suppose—that their candidate has no real chance of winning, and accordingly vote tactically for that one of the other two whom they prefer. It happens far more seldom that supporters of the second most popular candidate—the one who would receive the second highest total of votes if voting was sincere—realize that *their* candidate has no real chance of winning; yet, even by our severe criterion, it may be so. Let us change the example to see how this might have been so. This time, suppose that, if all had voted sincerely, the results would have been:

B: 18,668
C: 24,033
A: 12,434

C would have won under sincere voting in this case too. Did B have a chance of winning? By our criterion, he would have had no chance of doing so if the number of voters who preferred him to C was less than 24,033, that is, if the number of A's supporters who preferred B to C was less than 5,365. Suppose that it was: let us assume that just 4,900 of A's supporters preferred B to C. Then, even if *all* of these had switched their votes to B, while everyone else voted sincerely, C would still have won.

Could A have won? To do so, he would have needed at least 11,600 votes in addition to those of his supporters; but this is not impossible. If 12,003 of B's supporters, preferring A to C, had switched their votes to A, all other electors voting sincerely, the result would have been:

B: 6,665
C: 24,033
A: 24,437

and A would have won. In a familiar type of case, it is not at all unlikely that as many as 12,003 of B's 18,668 supporters should prefer **A** to **C**. This might well happen if **A** occupied a political position intermediate between **B** and **C**: those who favour the representative of one extreme position are likely to prefer a moderate to the representative of the other extreme position. What is unlikely is that so large a number of **B**'s supporters should have perceived that he had no real chance of winning, and that therefore their best tactic was to vote for **A**. It is more likely in practice that some of **A**'s supporters would have been tempted to vote tactically for **B**; but, if they had done so, their tactics would have been very ill judged.

If, in this case, **A** had won, would this have been a fair result, or ought **C** to have been the victor? We must answer this in the same way as we answered the parallel question in the previous example, whether **C** or **B** ought to have won, namely by asking, in the present case, whether a majority of the electorate preferred **C** to **A** or **A** to **C**. If at least 15,134 of **B**'s 18,668 supporters preferred **A** to **C**, then this would have been true also of a majority of the whole electorate; on the assumption that **A** occupies an intermediate political position between **B** and **C**, the supposition is quite possible. But if fewer than that number of **B**'s 18,668 supporters preferred **A** to **C**, a majority of the electorate would have preferred **C** to **A**, and it would be **C** who ought to have won.

We must conclude that the plurality system does not always deliver the right outcome—the election of the most representative candidate—when everyone votes sincerely. In both examples, **C** would have won in such a case; he may have been the most representative candidate, but, equally, he may not. By this standard, therefore, the plurality system is a very imperfect mechanism. But its imperfections are far from being sure to be corrected by tactical voting, for the system does not always deliver the right outcome when some vote tactically. In the first of our two examples, **B** won as a result of tactical voting: he may in fact have been the most representative candidate, but, again, he may not.

Suppose that, in our first example, **C** *was* the most representative candidate. Then, if sufficiently many of those of **A**'s supporters who preferred **C** to **B** had voted tactically for **C**, **C** would have won after all. But now suppose that **B** was the most representative candidate. It is still true, under this supposition, that, if sufficiently many of **A**'s supporters had voted tactically for **C**, he would have won.

Similar considerations apply to the second example. In the unlikely event of sufficiently many of **B**'s supporters voting tactically for **A**, **A** might well have won; again, he might have been the most representative candidate, or he might not. Likewise, tactical voting by those of **B**'s supporters who preferred **A** to **C** might have been blocked by tactical voting by others of his supporters who preferred **C**.

If there is no one candidate who commands the support of a majority of the electors, there can be little certainty what the outcome of the election will be under the plurality system: it depends on how many of the electors, and which of them, opt to vote tactically. They will decide this on the basis, not only of their own preferences, but of their highly fallible estimates of the preferences and probable tactics of other electors. If we are presented with the results of an election, we have no way of telling how many electors voted tactically. Even were we to be told, in addition, what the results would have been under sincere voting, we still cannot tell whether the successful candidate was the one who would best represent the constituency: the electors are not given sufficient opportunity to express their preferences either for us to tell what those preferences were or for the electors to make a well-informed decision how to cast their votes.

CHAPTER 6

Majority Preferences

IN the last chapter we first examined the case of a constituency election with three candidates in which, under the plurality system, **B** won, with some electors voting tactically, but in which, if all the electors had voted for the candidate of their first choice, **C** would have won. We asked which was the fairer outcome: which of these two candidates was the truest representative of the constituency? We answered by considering which of the two was preferred to the other by a majority of the electors: in other words, what the outcome would have been if the third candidate, **A**, had dropped out or been disqualified before the election. We then considered a second case, in which, had all voted sincerely, **C** would again have won, but in which, with some very judicious tactical voting, **A** might have won. We asked whether, in this second case, **A** or **C** ought to have been the winner; and we once more answered by considering which of the two was preferred to the other by a majority of the electors.

This appears reasonable. If, after the election, the voters had learned that a majority of them would have preferred another candidate, they would have been strongly disposed to judge that the result was unfair: that one of the defeated candidates would have represented them better than the one they had elected as their MP. Suppose, for example, that if C and B had been the only candidates, B would have won. Why, then, should the intervention of A be allowed to make a difference, giving the victory to C, as would have happened if all had then voted for their favourite candidates?

We used a similar technique in judging, in the first example, whether A had had any chance of winning, and hence to gauge the likelihood that his supporters would vote tactically. For that purpose, we compared the number of electors whose first choice was C with the number of those who preferred A to C—who would vote for A if B dropped out. We used the same technique in the second example, to decide whether B had a real chance of winning: in that case we compared the number of electors whose first choice was C with the number of those who preferred B to C. We have been engaged in *comparing candidates in pairs* to determine which of them is preferred by a majority of the electorate. We have done this both to judge the probability of tactical voting and the chances of its success, and to determine which is the most representative candidate.

For the former purpose it is indispensable; for the latter it is highly plausible. The notion of comparisons in pairs was used by the mathematician, encyclopaedist, and revolutionary the Marquis de Condorcet, who, in the years immediately preceding the French Revolution, was one of the first in modern times to make a systematic study of the theory of voting. We may assume that, of any two candidates in an election, one will be preferred to the other by a majority of the electors; the chances of an exact tie are too remote to be considered. Among any number of candidates, there may be one who is preferred by a majority to *each* of the other candidates, taken separately: in such a case, that one, according to Condorcet, deserves to be elected. Such a candidate is usually called a 'Condorcet winner', but the term is not altogether fortunate because, under many electoral systems, he may well not win; we may call him a 'Condorcet leader' instead. A candidate who is preferred to *all* the other candidates by a majority of the electors—who is the first choice of a majority—is obviously a Condorcet leader; in other cases, it will be a different majority that prefers the Condorcet leader to each different rival candidate. Iain McLean has discovered that, in proposing this criterion, Condorcet was anticipated by Ramon Lull in the thirteenth century.

The reason for accepting the opinion of Condorcet and Lull is very strong. If there is a Condorcet leader, then, whichever other candidate may be elected, it will be possible to complain that a majority of the electors would have preferred the Condorcet leader: the election will then almost certainly be judged to have had an unfair result by everyone who realizes what has happened.

In the first example of Chapter 5, either **C** or **B** could have been a Condorcet leader, and, in the second example, either **C** or **A** could have been: to the identity of the Condorcet leader a knowledge of which of the candidates commands the greatest number of electors whose first choice he is provides a very poor clue. They may of course be the same, as, under certain assumptions, **C** may have been in either of the examples of Chapter 5. But in other cases, the Condorcet leader may be a different candidate from the one who would win under the plurality system when everyone voted sincerely. There are two well-known situations in which this is particularly likely to happen. One is that known as a 'split opposition'. A highly controversial candidate has a large number of supporters, more than a third of the electorate but less than a half, and so not a majority. The majority of the electorate is strongly opposed to him, but divides its support between two other candidates, so that neither of them has as many supporters as the controversial candidate. The supporters of each of the opposition candidates would prefer the other opposition candidate to the controversial one. As a result, the controversial candidate, so far from being a Condorcet leader, is the opposite, which we may call a Condorcet tail: each of the other two candidates is preferred by a majority to him. One of those two other candidates will then be a Condorcet leader, that one, namely, who is the less disliked by the supporters of the controversial one. Plainly, he will merit election, rather than the controversial candidate, who will be elected under the plurality system if everyone votes sincerely, or if the supporters of the opposition candidates fail to get together and decide for which of them they will vote tactically.

The other familiar type of case is that in which there are two candidates representing relatively extreme opinions, with a third, moderate, candidate occupying an intermediate position. The moderate, candidate may well be the first choice of fewer electors than either of the more extreme ones. Yet, if none of the three commands an absolute majority of the electors, it is probable that the moderate candidate will be a Condorcet leader. This is because most of the supporters of either of the extreme candidates are likely to prefer the moderate candidate to the other extreme candidate. Since the supporters of any two of the candidates must form a majority, it follows that to each of the extreme candidates a majority will prefer the moderate one: he will therefore be the Condorcet leader.

In such a case, the thesis that the Condorcet leader ought to be elected is highly convincing. Although fewer electors regard him as the best of the three than so regard either of the other two, he is surely far more representative of opinion in the constituency than either of them. Opinion in the constituency is divided: to elect either of the extreme candidates, neither of whom commands majority support, when a majority would prefer the moderate, would be to choose someone who represented only one section of the electorate, not the electorate as a whole. In a case such as this, Condorcet's criterion selects, as the one who ought to be elected, a compromise candidate, in the true spirit of democracy. Some readers may be at first inclined to protest that it would not be right to elect a candidate who was the first choice of fewer voters than either of his rivals. But against this must be set the fact that he is rated the *worst* candidate by fewer voters than is either of the other two. Possibly he is thought to be the worst by none of the voters, whereas there are plenty who think one extreme candidate to be the worst, and plenty who think the same of the other.

The idea that what should primarily count in determining which candidate deserves election is the number of voters who think each candidate the best is very influential, especially in Britain and the United States. It arises chiefly because the plurality system now in use in both countries makes their electorates so familiar with it as the determining factor. Impartial reflection shows that the number of voters who think each candidate the worst (or the worst of the serious candidates) is no less important. No *more* important, either, indeed. A reverse system has been seriously proposed, under which each voter would place a cross against the name of the candidate he liked least, the candidate getting the lowest total being elected. People accustomed to this reverse system would tend to believe that the decisive factor should be how many voters regard a given candidate as the worst; they would be mystified by the idea that, in the case imagined, the moderate candidate was not obviously the one who ought to be elected. The reverse system is, of course, quite as fallacious as the plurality system. Both are based on a criterion for the most representative candidate that takes account of only a single aspect of voters' preferences. Condorcet's view was that the right criterion is one that takes a comprehensive account of voters' preferences as a whole. According to it, what matters is which, out of each pair of candidates, a majority prefers to the other. By relying on this criterion, we take simultaneous account *both* of how many think each candidate the best *and* of how many think each candidate the worst, and also, when there are more than three candidates, of other features of the voters' preferences besides. How can such a criterion fail to be superior to one that pays attention only to a restricted feature of those preferences?

Our conclusion about the moderate candidate and the two extreme ones can be generalized, a fact first observed by Duncan Black. Suppose that there are a number of candidates, who can all be ranged on a single scale of opinion from one extreme to another, for example, from Left to Right; say a Marxist, a Socialist, a Social Democrat, a

Radical, a Conservative, and a Fascist. Let us assume that every voter prefers a candidate to one side of the one he favours to every candidate further from the one he favours on the same side of him. If, for instance, he most favours the Social Democrat, he will prefer the Radical to the Conservative and the latter to the Fascist; he will also prefer the Socialist to the Marxist. Then there will be a Condorcet leader, and, if none of the candidates enjoys majority support, he will be one of the candidates occupying an intermediate position on the scale. We can identify the Condorcet leader in the following way. We start at one end of the scale, and move along it until we first arrive at a candidate whose supporters, together with the supporters of all the other candidates to the same side of him as the end from which we started, form a majority: he will be the Condorcet leader (it will make no difference from which end we start).

An example may make this clearer. Six candidates can be ranged from Left to Right in the order M, S, D, R, C, F, being, respectively, a Marxist, a Socialist, a Social Democrat, a Radical, a Conservative, and a Fascist. Out of an electorate of 6,000, the number of supporters of each are as follows:

M	S	D	R	C	F
300	1,700	1,100	1,500	1,200	200

If we start from the left, we shall find D to be the Condorcet leader, since his supporters and those of the candidates to his left (S and M) amount to a majority (3,100 out of 6,000), whereas this is not true of S, nor, of course, of M. By hypothesis, these 3,100 voters all prefer D to any of the three candidates to **D**'s right. Equally, the supporters of **D** and of the candidates to his right (**R**, **C** and **F**) form a majority (4,000 out of 6,000), whereas this is not true of **R**, nor, therefore, of **C** or **F**. By hypothesis, again, these 4,000 voters all prefer **D** to either of the two candidates, **S** and **M**, to **D**'s left.

In a case of this kind, the Condorcet leader may possibly have rather few supporters; but he will be the best compromise candidate who could be chosen. Of course, it is not very likely that literally *every* voter will have preferences between the candidates in accordance with the principle we have assumed; but a relatively small number of deviants will not disturb the conclusion.

Though extremely unlikely in practice, it is in theory possible, when there are at least four candidates, for one of them to be a Condorcet leader without being thought to be the best by a single voter. Suppose that support is divided between **A**, **B**, and **C**, none of whom commands a majority; but suppose also that **D** is the second choice of *every* voter. Then clearly **D** is the Condorcet leader; for the supporters of any two of the others will constitute a majority, which majority must prefer **D** to the remaining candidate. This is an extreme and improbable case; but it illustrates the fact that the number of voters regarding each candidate as their first choice is a hopelessly uncertain guide to which of them satisfies Condorcet's criterion. It is also a test of whether one really does accept that criterion. If, on reflection, you genuinely think it to be the right criterion for the most representative candidate, you must be prepared to agree that, in this bizarre case, **D** would deserve election. Some people may think that it would be going too far actually to elect someone whom no one thought to be the best of those standing; they then do not whole-heartedly accept the Condorcet criterion. But there are strong grounds for thinking that that would be a mistake. We have again a situation in which opinion is divided: **D** is the only possible compromise candidate; a majority would prefer him to any other that might be elected; and no one will be deeply dissatisfied with him.

It thus appears that we have found the answer to our question (1A): what should be the criterion, based on voters' actual preferences, for the most representative candidate? The criterion that forces itself upon us is that the most representative candidate is the Condorcet leader. This can be no more than half the answer, since we have been confining ourselves to elections to single-member constituencies; majorities have less obvious relevance to multi-member constituencies, which we have yet to consider. In the next chapter, we shall find, unhappily, that the Condorcet criterion is in need of supplementation; for the present, let us provisionally accept it.

From a solution to question (1A) for single-member constituencies, we should proceed to question (1B) for single-member constituencies: what electoral system will usually result in the election of the most representative candidate? In Chapter 2, we saw that the way to approach such a question was by first selecting a system that would yield the desired result whenever all the voters voted sincerely, and then to check how much incentive it offered for tactical voting, modifying it, if necessary, in order to reduce the incentive. In the present case, the problem appears straightforward. The voters must be asked to rank all the candidates in order of preference by placing numbers against their names (1 for the candidate the voter prefers to all others, 2 for his second choice, and so on). The ballot papers will then be scrutinized to determine if any candidate satisfies our criterion, so far as the ballot-papers show. A candidate will be declared to have won the election if, when compared in turn with every other candidate, taken separately, he proves to have been ranked higher than that other candidate by a majority of the electors. We may now rightly call such a candidate a 'Condorcet winner' since, under this system, he has genuinely won. If all have voted sincerely, he is the Condorcet leader, whom we hoped to identify and to elect under this system. As usual, we cannot be totally certain that he is in fact the Condorcet leader, because we cannot be certain that there has been no tactical voting; but there will be a strong probability that he is. The system itself may be called the (pairwise) comparison system.

Tactical voting appears to pose little threat to the comparison system, for it can never be to the advantage of any voter or group of voters to render some candidate the Condorcet winner who is not in fact the Condorcet leader. Suppose that some candidate A is the Condorcet leader, so that, if all vote sincerely, he will win. Another candidate, B, can become Condorcet winner only if a number of voters insincerely rank him above A. But this they can have no incentive to do, since, by hypothesis, they in fact prefer A to B; voters who really prefer B to A can have no effect on the majority preference for A over B.

The comparison system has a further desirable feature. Provided the electors do not change their rankings of the candidates, a Condorcet winner will remain a Condorcet winner if one of the candidates withdraws before the election; the system is therefore stable in that, if the election has to be held a second time because one of the unsuccessful candidates has been disqualified, the result will be the same as before.

We thus appear to have arrived at an ideal system for holding elections to single-member constituencies.

CHAPTER 7

Rival Criteria

THE optimistic conclusion of the last chapter seems too good to be true. Unhappily, it *is* too good to be true.

Individual preferences must be transitive. By this technical term it is simply meant that if an individual voter prefers A to B and B to C, he must prefer A to C: it would be quite irrational of him to claim to prefer C to A. But the same does not hold for majority preferences. They are sometimes *intransitive*: out of any set of voters, it may be that A is preferred to B by a majority of them, B to C by a different majority of them, and C to A by yet another majority of them. This so-called 'paradox of voting' is the fundamental fact of the theory of voting. It almost always comes as a great surprise to anyone who learns of it for the first time; but, once one has been told that it is so, it is easy to verify that it is indeed so. Suppose that our set of voters can be divided into three equal groups, sharing the same preferences between the candidates within each group; any two groups will together form a majority. A majority prefers A to B: so suppose this preference is shared by members of groups 1 and 2. A different majority prefers B to C; so suppose that this preference is shared by members of groups 1 and 3. We now know the full preferences of members of group 1: they all prefer **A** to **B** and **B** to **C**. Finally, a majority prefers **C** to **A**: this must be composed of the members of groups 2 and 3. Thus members of group 2 all prefer **C** to **A** and **A** to **B**, while members of group 3 all prefer **B** to **C** and **C** to **A**. We have constructed an example of intransitive majority preferences, without violating the transitivity of individual preferences. We did not need to postulate that the three groups were equal in number: indeed, it was sufficient that each contained less than half the total number of voters.

That majority preferences should be intransitive is not a rare occurrence that we can safely ignore, but quite a common one. The intransitivity of majority preference is the source of all the unwelcome facts about voting, and of all the difficulty of the subject. Among the unwelcome facts is one that has already been mentioned, that it is in principle impossible to devise an electoral system that will never offer any advantage to tactical voting. We seemed to have discovered a counter-example to this in the comparison system; but that was only because we were ignoring the possibility that the majority preferences might be intransitive. This possibility implies that there may not be a Condorcet leader; when the majority preferences are transitive, there is bound to be one. The existence of a cycle of majority preferences will not always have this effect. If the majority preferences between **A**, **B**, and **C** are intransitive, but a fourth candidate, **D**, is preferred by a majority to each of them, then **D** will be a Condorcet leader; the intransitive majorities between the other three will make no difference. But if **D** is *not* preferred by a majority to each of the other three, or if those three are the only candidates, then, plainly, there will be no Condorcet leader. When there is no Condorcet leader, it will follow that, *whoever* is elected, it will be true to say, of at least one other candidate, that a majority would have preferred him. This fact does not, therefore, establish conclusively that the outcome of the election was unfair.

The comparison system is thus incomplete: it needs supplementing by a means of determining the outcome when the ballot papers fail to yield a Condorcet winner. On the means of supplementation will depend what chances there are for tactical voting. Sometimes it will be possible to argue, on the basis of majority preferences alone, that a particular candidate would be the most representative. Suppose that there are five candidates, E to I, of whom F is preferred by a majority to E, while E is preferred by a majority to each of the other three. These three form a cycle (G is preferred by a majority to H, H to I, and I to G); but each of them is preferred by a majority to F. Such a distribution of majority preferences is perfectly possible; in fact, any assumption about majority preferences can be realized by a suitable allocation of preference scales to the voters. In the case imagined, it can be argued that E is the most representative candidate and ought to be elected. Admittedly, if he is, it will be possible to say that a majority would have preferred F; but, if F had been elected, it would have been possible to say this about each of three other candidates, while, if any of those three had been elected, it would have been possible to say it about either of two others (E being one of them).

If majority preferences are regarded as an important guide to how representative of the constituency a candidate may be, then, when there is no Condorcet leader, we may consider each candidate's *Copeland number*, being the number of other candidates to whom he is preferred by a majority. (This idea was first suggested by A. H. Copeland in his 1957 paper, 'A "reasonable" social welfare function'.) Thus, in the case imagined, E has a Copeland number of 3, F of 1, and G, H, and I Copeland numbers of 2 each. We might then lay it down, as a partial criterion for determining the most representative candidate, that a candidate could be regarded as representative only if he had a Copeland number at least as high as that of any other candidate. In the foregoing case, this criterion would pick E as the only representative candidate, since he has a higher Copeland number than any of the other four. This new criterion is a generalization of the principle that a Condorcet leader must be the most representative candidate, since a Condorcet leader will always have the highest Copeland number, namely the total number of candidates minus 1.

The generalized criterion will not always pick a single candidate as the most representative. Suppose that, in the above example, I withdraws before the election, so that there are now only four candidates. In this altered situation, E and G will each have a Copeland number of 2, while F and H have Copeland numbers of 1 each. The criterion rules out F and H, but allows G as well as E to be considered a representative candidate. Of course, if there are only three candidates and no Condorcet leader, each will have a Copeland number of 1, and the criterion will not rule out any of them.

This suggests a partial modification to the comparison system. From the ballot-papers, each candidate's *Copeland score* will be calculated, being the number of other candidates above whom that candidate is ranked by a majority (his Copeland *number* is based on the voters' real preferences, his

Copeland *score* on what is shown on the ballot-papers). If there is a candidate with a Copeland score higher than every other candidate's, he will be declared elected. Otherwise some supplementary means will be needed to choose between those candidates whose Copeland scores are higher than all the others'.

Such a means lies to hand in the method of election proposed by another French mathematician, Jean-Charles de Borda, a contemporary of Condorcet and another pioneer in the theory of voting. As Iain McLean has discovered, it was also proposed, for the election of the Emperor, by Nicholas of Cusa in about 1434. The method proposed by Borda and Nicholas of Cusa may again be explained in terms of comparisons by pairs. Given the preferences of the voters, we again imagine that each candidate is pitted against each of the others taken in turn. This time, however, we take account, not just of which out of a pair of candidates beats the other in the contest between them, but of the number of votes that would be cast for each if all voted sincerely. For each candidate, we add together all the votes cast for him in all his contests with other candidates, regardless of which of them he won and which he lost. The grand total is his *Borda count*. This suggests a rival criterion for which candidate should be considered the most representative. Ignoring majority preferences, we might hold the most representative candidate the one who has the highest Borda count. Alternatively, we might continue to adhere to the Copeland number criterion, using Borda's criterion merely as supplementary. In this case we shall regard as the most representative candidate to be that one, out of those having a Copeland number at least as high as that of any other candidate, who has the highest Borda count. Yet again, we might reject the idea of Copeland numbers, but still adhere to the straightforward criterion of Condorcet, when applicable. We should then take the most representative candidate to be the Condorcet leader, if there is one, and otherwise the one having the highest Borda count.

The principle underlying Borda's criterion for the most representative single candidate is that majorities are of no importance in themselves; rather, every preference felt by any voter for any one candidate over another should count, and count equally to every other such preference. An obvious objection is that they are not all of equal strength. The answer is that, while they are not all of equal strength, there is no general rule to determine where, so to speak, the biggest gaps will come in a voter's preference scale. Some voters will be committed to a particular political party. They will probably greatly prefer the candidate of that party to any other, and feel only mild preferences between candidates of other parties. Other voters will care intensely that the candidate of a certain party should be defeated, and feel only mild preferences between candidates of parties they prefer to his. Yet others may feel only a slight preference for the candidate of their first choice out of four over the one of their second choice, and for the candidate of their third choice over the one they like least, while strongly preferring the candidate of their second choice to the one of their third choice. The only solution, given that we do not know the strengths of voters' preferences, and that there is no practicable way of discovering them, is to treat all preferences as equal, on the principle that, across a large electorate, the inaccuracies will cancel out.

An alternative way to look at Borda's criterion is to see it
as, precisely, a rough method of estimating the strength of
voters' preferences. This is derived from an alternative way
of explaining Borda counts. For each voter's preference
scale, we assign 0 points to the candidate he ranks lowest, 1
point to the candidate he ranks lowest but one, 2 points to
the one he ranks lowest but two, and so on up; if there are
six candidates, the one he ranks highest will receive 5 points.
The total of points acquired by each candidate from all the
voters taken together will be his Borda count. It needs only
a little thought to see that this method of reckoning Borda
counts is equivalent to that given previously. Now suppose
that there are six candidates, and that a particular voter
ranks **B** second highest and **E** lowest but one. Then he will
contribute 4 points to **B**'s Borda count and only 1 point to
E's. The difference of 3 points between them reflects the
fact that the voter quite strongly prefers **B** to **E**: his placing
two candidates between them on his preference scale indicates that his preference is relatively strong.

If there is a Condorcet leader, he will, more often than
not, have the highest Borda count. He will not do so
in every case, however: Condorcet's criterion and that of
Borda by no means always coincide. We have seen that
Condorcet's criterion disadvantages controversial candidates. It will not, however, disadvantage a controversial candidate who commands majority support, for he will then of
course be a Condorcet leader. Borda's criterion will sometimes disadvantage even such a candidate. The point may be
illustrated, for simplicity, by a highly schematic example, in
which the unlikely assumption is made that the supporters
of each candidate share exactly the same preference scales;

naturally, the point does not *depend* upon assuming such a regular set of preferences. Suppose that there are 56,000 electors and four candidates, **A**, **B**, **C**, and **D**. **A** is a highly controversial candidate, supported by 29,000 of the electors but regarded as the least desirable by 25,000 of them. As shown on the diagram below, the 29,000 supporters of **A** rank the candidates in the order **A, B, C, D**. The 24,000 supporters of **B** rank them in the order **B, C, D, A**. There are 2,000 supporters of **C**, who rank the candidates in the order **C, A, B, D**. Finally, the 1,000 supporters of **D** rank them in the order **D, C, B, A**.

29,000	24,000	2,000	1,000
A	B	C	D
B	C	A	C
C	D	B	B
D	A	D	A

Under the plurality system, A's majority of 5,000—the gap between his votes and those of **B**—would be considered fairly robust; he would also be elected under the comparison system, having an absolute majority of 2,000 over the other candidates combined. Yet B's Borda count of 133,000 is higher than A's of 91,000; **C** obtains a Borda count of 85,000 and **D** one of 27,000. There is undoubtedly a case to be made for saying that **B** is a more representative candidate than **A**. All of A's supporters reckon him the second-best candidate, and no elector thinks him the worst: he would surely represent opinion in the constituency better than **A**.

It would be wrong to conclude from this that Borda's criterion favours bland, insipid candidates: on the contrary, it treats both contentious and mediocre candidates even-handedly. A candidate who occupies the middle position in every elector's preference scale will obtain just the same Borda count as one who is rated the best by exactly half the electors and the worst by the other half, that is, an average Borda count; unless all candidates have just the same Borda count, neither of the two can have the highest.

We are still trying to answer question (1A) for single-member constituencies: on the basis of the electors' true preferences, which single candidate is the most representa-tive? We need an answer to this question in order that we may assess how far different electoral systems can be relied on to produce the outcome that is to be desired. Had it not been for the possible intransitivity of majority preferences, we should have had a highly plausible answer: the Condorcet leader. As it is, we need a supplementary crite-rion for cases in which there is no Condorcet leader. The Copeland number criterion provides a partial supplementa-tion; but we still need further supplementation for cases which that criterion fails to decide completely. The only such supplementary criterion that is at all persuasive is Borda's; and that makes a claim to be, not merely a supple-mentary criterion, but, rather, the sole criterion.

It is up to the reader to judge between the competing claims. Borda's criterion and that of Condorcet, together with Copeland's extension of the second of the two, appear to me to be the only plausible criteria ever suggested for which one candidate, out of a number, would best represent the electors. There can be no actual proof of this contention. To give a proof, we should need already to have at our com-mand a precise criterion for the most representative candidate, and show that it tallied with either Condorcet's or Borda's criterion; but it is just such a criterion that we are seeking.

There might, however, be a plausible argument for the contention.* The basis for the judgement which of the candidates is the most representative is the set of rankings in order of preference of those candidates by the individual electors. Suppose that we were concerned, not merely to identify the *one* most representative candidate, but to draw up a master ranking of the candidates in order of their representativeness. This master ranking would be a resultant of all the individual rankings: it would come as close as any single ranking could to the various individual rankings. If we could identify such a master ranking, we should have a highly plausible identification of the most representative candidate, namely the one highest in the master ranking.

We need a measure of the 'distance' between any one ranking and another, that is, the degree to which they differ. One such measure might be found by treating as 1 unit of distance apart any two rankings which can be obtained from one another by interchanging two adjacent candidates, leaving the rest as they are: thus, when there are four candidates, the distance between **ABCD** and **ACBD** is 1 by this measure. The distance between any two rankings whatever would then be the length of the shortest path from one to the other, a step on the path being of length 1 and the length of the path the number of steps along it. Thus the distance between **ABCD** and **DCBA** would be 6 by this measure, one of the shortest paths from the former to the latter being **BACD, BCAD, BCDA, BDCA, DBCA, DCBA**.

* This line of thought was suggested to me by a referee.

Given this measure of distance between rankings, how should the master ranking, if there is one, be identified? We might define the 'total distance' of any ranking as the sum of its distances from the rankings of the individual electors; the master ranking is that whose total distance is least. If there is a 'Condorcet ranking', that will be the master ranking. A Condorcet ranking of four candidates will be one in which the first is preferred by a majority to each of the others and thus is the Condorcet leader, the second is preferred by a majority to each of the remaining two, and the third is preferred by a majority to the fourth; in other words the first has a Copeland number of 3, the second of 2, the third of 1, and the fourth of 0. There may not be a Condorcet ranking, but still a Condorcet leader, namely if there is a cycle of majority preferences among the other three candidates: in this case the Condorcet leader will have a Copeland number of 3, and the remaining three will each have a Copeland number of 1. In such a case, there may be no single master ranking, but two or more 'best rankings', each of them being at the same total distance, this being smaller than the total distance of any ranking other than them. The Condorcet leader will be highest in each of these best rankings. In general, the Condorcet leader, if there is one, will always be highest in any best ranking.

This does not establish that Condorcet's criterion, whenever applicable, will always select the most representative candidate, since there are other ways in which we might carry out a similar test. For instance, using the same measure of distance between rankings as before, we might define the total distance of a given ranking from the individual rankings as the sum of the *squares* of its distances from them. When the total distance is defined in this way, then, in most (though not quite all) cases in which there is a Condorcet leader, but some other candidate has the highest Borda count, the master ranking will rank highest the candidate with the highest Borda count rather than the Condorcet leader. Again, the distance between rankings might be measured differently: for instance, as the sum of the number of places each candidate is shifted from one ranking to the other. A convincing argument for the contention that the two criteria, Borda's and Condorcet's (perhaps generalized by Copeland's), are the only plausible ones for selecting the most representative candidate would consist in showing that, however the distance between two rankings was defined, and however total distance was then defined in terms of it, any best ranking must have in its highest place either a candidate with the highest Copeland number or one with the highest Borda count. Tests on sample cases render this extremely likely, but a general proof of it would be difficult and will not be attempted here.

Enough has been said in this book to show that being the first choice of more voters than any other candidate is *not* a plausible criterion for being the most representative candidate. If readers are disposed to propose some criterion other than the two we are considering, they should test out their intuitions. The way to test them is by constructing hypothetical examples in which the proposed criterion conflicts with both Condorcet's and Borda's; contemplating such examples, they must ask themselves whether the candidate selected by their criterion really is more representative than the one selected by one or other of those we have been considering. If they remain convinced that he is, they may be able to reinforce his claim by devising a measure of distance between rankings, or a definition of total distance, under which the master ranking will rank highest the candidate satisfying their criterion. My personal belief is that no such rival criterion can be devised; but I must leave further reflection to the readers.

A reader who agrees that Condorcet's and Borda's criteria are the only plausible ones must still make up his mind between them for himself, since, once again, there can be no proof which is the sounder of the two. He should therefore ask himself whether, in determining which is the most representative candidate, the question whether more voters prefer one candidate to another is more or less important than how strong the preferences are, and more or less important than how often either candidate is preferred to some other. When he has decided by which criterion he is more attracted, he should again construct problem cases and reflect on them. Problem cases are those in which some candidate has the support of a majority of the electors, but does not have the highest Borda count, as in the example above; those in which a candidate is a Condorcet leader, although not having the support of a majority, but again does not have the highest Borda count; and ones in which a candidate, though not a Condorcet leader, has as high a Copeland number as any other candidate, but has a lower Borda count than some candidate with a smaller Copeland number. Readers uncertain to which criterion they should adhere are recommended to try their hand at constructing examples of these three kinds, and then reflect carefully on which of the candidates their intuition tells them is the most representative of the electors.

It seems clear that Borda's criterion is the soundest method of identifying the candidate who is most generally popular with the electorate, or at least the most acceptable. To some minds, that fact will be conclusive: what else could we be after when we ask for the 'most representative' candidate? But others will attach a special importance to majorities; and to them Condorcet's criterion, and its generalization, the Copeland number criterion, will appeal. Even though some candidate, **J**, had the highest Borda count, it would seem unjust to them were he to be elected, while another candidate, **B**, was Condorcet leader. **J** may have been the most generally popular candidate; but a majority would have preferred **B**, and this, to those who think in this way, will seem, in such a case, to be decisive. They are captivated, as many people are, by what may be called the mystique of the majority; it is often thought to be the foundation of democracy that the will of a majority should be paramount.

It is *not* the foundation of democracy, however; this is, rather, that the rights of minorities should be protected. You will hear people say, 'A majority was in favour: that's democratic, isn't it?' The only correct answer is 'Not necessarily.' Even if there were only two options, the question is whether that favoured by the majority was oppressive to the minority, and, if so, whether that favoured by the minority would have been equally oppressive to the majority; it must also be asked whether no compromise was possible. The power exerted by the mystique of the majority is very largely due to the fact that many of the most familiar voting systems—though not the plurality system, of course—embody a principle of determining the outcome by a majority. Under some systems, the majority is factitious, arrived at by some process of eliminating some of the candidates or possible outcomes; but their advocates claim that the outcome represents the will of the majority, and so the idea is implanted that the preference of a majority is essential to deciding what it is that democratic principles require.

It does not in the end matter where the idea comes from; the serious question is: is it valid? Does one candidate's being preferred by a majority to another tell decisively in favour of the first's claim to be elected, even if the second candidate has greater general popularity? Many will feel a strong inclination to answer 'Yes'; but no one can reasonably give this answer without qualification, since majority preferences may be intransitive, and the two candidates part of a cycle of three. The answer, 'Yes, in the absence of any problem due to intransitivity of majority preferences' has a less convincing ring. Perhaps the better way to ask the question is: how much does it matter that, if possible, it can be said that there is no other particular candidate whom a majority would have preferred to the one who was elected? How much does it matter, given that it is not always possible to say this, whoever is elected? There would be no point in expressing an opinion in this book about how much it matters: readers must make up their own minds.

It may be of help to readers, in trying to decide between Borda's and Condorcet's criteria, to provide two last examples, each with 11,000 voters, in which those criteria differ; these may also help them to see if they can devise other criteria, or, by modifying the examples, to construct one in which the candidate whose claim to be representative is most plausible satisfies neither Borda's criterion nor Condorcet's.

In the first example, the voters' preferences are as follows:

1,000	5,000	5,000
A	B	C
B	A	D
C	C	E
D	D	A
E	E	B

	A	B	C	D	E
Copeland number	4	3	2	1	0
Borda count	24,000	23,000	32,000	21,000	1,0000
ranked highest by	1,000	5,000	5,000	0	0
ranked lowest by	0	5,000	0	0	6,000

A is the Condorcet leader; C has the highest Borda count. The second example is as follows:

1,000	4,000	1,000	4,000	1,000
A	A	B	B	C
B	C	A	C	D
C	D	C	D	E
D	E	D	E	A
E	B	E	A	B

	A	B	C	D	E
Copeland number	4	3	2	1	0
Borda count	24,000	23,000	32,000	21,000	10,000
ranked highest by	5,000	5,000	1,000	0	0
ranked lowest by	4,000	5,000	0	0	2,000

The reader will observe that, despite the different appearance of the two examples, the Copeland numbers and Borda counts are the same in each. The number of voters who rank each candidate highest is a poor guide to the candidate rated best on either of our two criteria, as is the number of voters who rank each candidate lowest. To express it in the converse manner, the candidate who is the first choice of the greatest number of voters will often not be Condorcet leader or have the highest Borda count; nor will the candidate ranked lowest by the smallest number of voters. Which criterion, in the reader's opinion—the two we have been considering, or some other—selects the candidate with the best claim to be the most representative? Does any plausible criterion select a candidate other than A or C? Can a different example be constructed in which a plausible criterion selects one who is neither Condorcet leader nor has the highest Borda count?

CHAPTER 8

Systems Based on Criteria

I N the last chapter, we considered an extension of Condorcet's criterion for the most representative single candidate, using the notion of a candidate's Copeland number, and also a new criterion, that proposed by Borda, either to supplement Condorcet's criterion or its extension, or else for use as the sole criterion. There are three electoral systems corresponding to these three criteria; under each of them, when all vote sincerely, the victory will go to the candidate satisfying the chosen criterion. The first is the pure *Borda system*. Under this, the voters are required to rank all the candidates in order of preference, as before. The Borda score of each candidate is then calculated, his Borda *score* being his Borda count, as estimated from the ballot-papers. The candidate having the highest Borda score is declared elected. The easiest way to compute the Borda scores is as follows. For each ballot-paper, the candidate ranked lowest by the voter is allotted no points; the one ranked just above him (second lowest) is allotted 1 point; the one ranked third lowest is allotted 2 points, and so on upwards. The sum of all the points any candidate receives from all the ballot papers together is his Borda score. It is important to grasp that this is not a mere extension of the comparison system.

As we saw in the last chapter, a Condorcet leader will, more often than not, have the highest Borda score; but he will not always do so. The Borda system will therefore not always lead to the election of the candidate who would have won under the comparison system.

The alternative is to use Borda scores as mere supplements to the comparison system. The simplest method, the *modified comparison system*, will be to treat the Condorcet winner, if one is found to exist, as having been elected, but, if there is none, to calculate the Borda scores, declaring the candidate with the highest score elected. In the first case, the result should be announced by stating the majority achieved by the Condorcet winner over each of the other candidates (in the sense of the difference between the number who would prefer him and the number who would prefer the other candidate); in the second case, the Borda scores of all the candidates would be announced. Pressure to announce the Borda scores when there was a Condorcet winner should, if possible, be resisted, in case some candidate other than the Condorcet winner had the highest Borda score; supporters of that candidate might well be disgruntled if they realized the fact. At worst, the Borda scores of the defeated candidates might be announced, but not that of the candidate who has been elected as being the Condorcet winner.

Here is a fact which it may be better for the voters *not* to know; but pressure to reveal it may be too strong to resist. The problem arises because the system is based on distinct criteria for the most deserving candidate, one needing to be supplemented by the other. The difficulty does not arise under the pure Borda system, since there is unlikely to be pressure to reveal the majority preferences; if there were, exactly the same embarrassment might arise. The Borda system will be approved by those who are satisfied that Borda's criterion is, by itself, a sound method of determining the most representative candidate, provided they do not consider the risk of tactical voting too great. It has the advantage of being simpler to explain, and of avoiding the possible embarrassment of a publicly known conflict between criteria. The danger of such embarrassment arises from the very nature of voting; but only a very sophisticated electorate will recognize its inevitability.

When Copeland scores are taken into account, we shall have what may be called the *composite system*. The voters again rank all the candidates in order of preference. Their Borda scores and their Copeland scores are calculated. The candidates who have lower Copeland scores than others are eliminated; of those remaining, that one with the highest Borda score is declared elected.

There are different ways in which the results could be announced under the composite system. They could be announced simply by giving separately the Copeland scores and Borda scores of all the candidates (voters would probably not tolerate the announcement of the Borda scores only of those candidates who had the highest Copeland scores). The disadvantage of this would be the psychological effect already discussed. Supporters of a candidate who had a lower Copeland score than the winner would be likely to be aggrieved if he had a higher Borda score, complaining that he had a better right to election. Another method would be to calculate *composite scores* for all the candidates. To each candidate's Borda score there would be added a bonus for every other candidate to whom he was preferred by a majority; the total would constitute the candidate's final or composite score. The size of the bonus would depend both on the number of candidates and the number of votes cast. These composite scores would be announced, and the candidate with the highest score declared elected. The amount of the bonus would have to be calculated so as to ensure that a candidate who had a Copeland score higher than another would always obtain a higher final score than that other candidate: in this way the system could guarantee both that a Condorcet winner, if any, would be elected, and that no candidate could be elected who had a lower Copeland score than some other candidate. Since the composite scores would be rather large, a further possibility would be to scale them down to make their sum equal the total number of votes cast, announcing only the scaled-down scores.

The principle of the bonuses would have, of course, to be explained to the electors. Nevertheless, the use of composite scores, scaled down or raw, would yield a uniform method of announcing the results, rather than by means of two separate figures. It remains that any elector, politician, or journalist who understood how the bonus was calculated could, if competent at arithmetic, resolve the composite scores into their component Copeland scores and Borda scores. Since, given the number of candidates and the number of voters, the sum total of the raw composite scores could be calculated, it would still be possible to extract both the Copeland scores and the Borda scores even if the composite scores were scaled down, by the simple process of first scaling up again.

In order to have the effect that a candidate will always

have a higher composite score than another if he has a higher Copeland score, the bonus can be calculated by multiplying the number of candidates minus 2 by half the number of votes cast, rounding down if this is odd. Thus if there are six candidates and 54,001 votes are cast, the bonus will be 108,000; a candidate with a Copeland score of 2 will have a composite score of 216,000 plus his Borda score. If Z has the highest possible Borda score consistent with his Copeland score, and Y has the lowest possible Borda score consistent with *his* Copeland score, which is 1 higher than Z's, Z's Borda score will be higher than Y's; but the bonus will be greater than the difference between them.

The bonus, so calculated, would usually be much larger than was actually necessary, and it would vary from election to election, since it depends on the size of the turnout. If it were thought acceptable, the tellers could determine, from the Copeland scores and Borda scores, the least size of bonus necessary for its intended purpose, which would sometimes be 0, and use this rather than that just defined. The bonus is not, after all, a measure of anything, but simply a device to ensure that superiority in Copeland scores overrides superiority in Borda scores. If this were done, the results, as announced, certainly ought to be scaled down. Provided that any pressure to reveal the value of the bonus was resisted, this procedure would solve the problem of voters' becoming aware of a conflict between the Copeland number criterion and the Borda criterion. Ignorance of the size of the bonus would frustrate the process of scaling up the scores as announced to obtain the raw composite scores, since it would not be known in advance what the sum total of the raw composite scores should be, and hence by what factor to scale up. It would then be immensely laborious, and perhaps impossible, to extract from the announced scores the original Copeland scores and Borda scores.

Those who accept Borda's criterion for the most representative candidate will be happy with the pure Borda system, at least if they are not afraid of the incentives it gives for tactical voting: results will be announced in a uniform manner, and it is unlikely that a conflict between the criteria will come to light. Readers disinclined to accept the Borda system may well be swayed to reject the composite system or the modified comparison system by their dismay at the dissatisfaction that may be caused when a conflict between the criteria is revealed when the results are announced. That is very natural; the dilemma is a disagreeable one. It has already been remarked, however, that a possible clash of criteria is not an artefact of any particular system, but lies in the nature of things. It is intrinsic to how preferences may be distributed that there can be a clash between the two criteria; it is intrinsic to it that a criterion based on majority preferences will not always pick out one candidate best by that criterion; it is likewise intrinsic to it that the only reasonable supplementary criterion is one that may conflict with it when it does pick out such a candidate.

What, in this situation, ought we to do? What is usually done is to adopt some electoral system, such as the plurality or the alternative vote system, which does not involve either majority preferences or aggregations of preferences (such as those given by Borda scores) in its mechanism. For that reason such a system will frequently result in the election of a candidate who is not by either criterion the one who ought to have been elected. We shall then rely on an unreflective impression on the part of electors that the system we have adopted is 'fair', and on the fact that it will be quite impossible to determine, from the results of any particular election, whether the outcome was fair or not in the sense that the candidate elected was the one who would best represent the constituency. The system will disguise the relevant facts; and so, by operating a system that is grossly unfair but is not manifestly so, we shall be spared the embarrassment of having to persuade dissatisfied voters that the criterion on which our system is founded is superior to that to which they are appealing. That is what is almost universally done in practice. It can hardly be what anyone who seriously wishes the electorate to be fairly represented would recommend.

We have no way of avoiding the difficulty under the modified comparison system; but a means of avoiding it under the composite system was suggested above. This will be effective provided voters are not determined to unearth any possible clash between the criteria. In any case, it may well be that anxiety about voters' resentment caused by a divergence between the two criteria is out of place. The public is deeply imbued with the mystique of the majority; it might therefore be well prepared to accept a Condorcet winner as the right candidate to have been elected, even though some other was known to have had a higher Borda score. The problem is not menacing enough to deter us from adopting the composite system if it appears to us more just than the Borda system or than any other; there will be time enough to think again if, once adopted, it should prove to generate grave disputes over whether or not it is fair.

We have yet to investigate what incentives these electoral

systems would give to tactical voting. We have seen that, under the comparison system, no set of voters can have both the capacity and the incentive to vote tactically with the effect that some candidate becomes the Cordorcet winner when, if everyone had voted sincerely, another candidate would have been. Suppose that, out of several candidates, **A** is the Condorcet leader: if all voted sincerely, he would be elected. How could a set of voters so list the candidates that another one, **B**, became Condorcet winner? Plainly, they would need to list **B** higher than **A**. Those of them who preferred **A** to **B**, and would have listed **A** higher if they had voted sincerely, may certainly change the outcome in this way: they might make **B** appear to be preferred to **A** by a majority, thus dethroning **A** from the status of Condorcet winner, and possibly causing **B** to win. Since these voters preferred **A** to **B**, however, they would have no incentive to do this. Voters who preferred **B** to **A** would have an incentive, but could not by this means make any change in the outcome: they would in any case have ranked **B** higher than **A**, and have no way of rendering **B**'s chances greater than those of **A**.

The comparison system is an incomplete procedure, however. When it is supplemented, first by a rule about Copeland scores and then by appeal to Borda scores, it becomes the composite system. The previous reasoning is now no longer compelling: voters may now have an incentive to vote tactically in order to reduce a candidate's Copeland score. Suppose that there are four candidates, and that, if all voted sincerely, **A** would be the Condorcet winner, **B** obtaining a Copeland score of 2, **C** one of 1, and **D** one of 0. Suppose further that a certain set of voters would, if they voted sincerely, rank the candidates in the order **B, C, A, D**. By voting tactically and ranking the candidates on their ballot papers in the order **B, C, D, A**, they may succeed in overturning **A**'s majority over **D**. In this case **A**'s Copeland score will be reduced from 3 to 2, and **D**'s increased from 0 to 1. **B** will now have a chance of winning: if he has a higher Borda score than **A**, he *will* win.

Such tactical voting is very uncertain. **A** may well have a higher Borda score than **B**, in which case the tactical voters will have made a difference to the results as announced, but not to who wins the election. It is also very perilous. If the tactical voters have not estimated the probable Copeland scores correctly, the effect of their tactical vote may well be to convert **D** into a Condorcet winner in place of **A**, a worse result for them than if they had voted sincerely. Tactical voting can benefit those who undertake it under the composite system, as it can under any system; but it will do so only if the tactical voters can make an accurate assessment of the Copeland scores of all the candidates (and not just merely of which candidate is likely to be a Condorcet winner), which is difficult to do. For this reason, it is unlikely to be undertaken very often. The composite system is not very vulnerable to tactical voting.

The pure Borda system has a very unusual feature. Almost every other electoral system that has ever been used or proposed has the property that it is capable of being *manipulated by a majority*, in the sense that, if a majority of voters together determine on bringing about the election of a particular candidate, they will have a means of so voting that that candidate will be elected, no matter how the others choose to cast their votes. Normally, this will involve the members of the majority all voting in the same way, but this is not part of the definition: all that is necessary is that there should be a way for each member of the majority to vote such that, if every member votes in the prescribed way, the agreed-on candidate will be elected. The Borda system is quite exceptional in that it cannot in this sense be manipulated by a majority. There is scope for tactical voting, indeed. If the voters in some set want to get a certain candidate elected, and decide that some other candidate is his only serious rival, they can try ranking their favoured candidate highest and the rival lowest, even though they actually prefer the rival to some of the other candidates; and the tactic may be successful. But even a majority of voters has no way of voting that will ensure that a given candidate will obtain the highest Borda score, however the remaining voters decide to fill in their ballot-papers. No majority can *impose* its will. This feature will be repugnant to those imbued with the mystique of the majority; it will be attractive to those who believe that minorities ought to have some say in what happens.

Under the Borda system, a voter who contemplates voting tactically in order to give his favourite candidate the best possible chance of being elected, and believes himself to be well informed about the preferences of the other voters, might well proceed as follows. He will first classify the candidates into those whom he believes to have a chance of success and those whom he thinks have no chance. He will then rank highest his favourite candidate among those he credits with a chance of success. After him he will set, in order of preference, those candidates he prefers to the one he has ranked highest; by hypothesis, he does not believe any of these to have a real chance of winning. Finally, he will rank below these, in inverse order of their estimated chances of winning, all those candidates to whom he prefers the one he has ranked highest. By this means, he will give the best possible chance to the candidate he has ranked highest.

Such a tactic is not desperately risky, and may have an effect favourable to the voter. If a certain number of voters adopt the same tactic, ranking the same candidate highest, they may succeed in securing for him the highest Borda score. If they do not succeed in this, the tactic may have an adverse effect by bringing about the election of a candidate they greatly disliked, especially if their estimates of the chances of success of the various candidates, under sincere voting, were unsound. But the tactic will work only if all but a small minority of voters vote sincerely. If a great many voters adopt a similar tactic in favour of other candidates, this will completely throw out any estimates of candidates' success, however sound. This is because the tactic requires candidates judged to have no real chance of success to be given high rankings; if many voters make similar estimates of the candidates' chances of success, estimates that would be sound if all voted sincerely, and vote tactically in accordance with the same recipe, they will convert candidates who had no chance of success into ones highly likely to win.

The Borda system offers a fair incentive to tactical voting; while its profitability demands a good judgement of the candidates' chances of success, based on a knowledge of other voters' intentions, it is, given that, reasonably obvious what the best tactics are, and not very hazardous to adopt them. The effect of a few voters' voting tactically will seldom be grave: they may replace the candidate who would have had the highest Borda score under sincere voting by one almost equally popular, but will seldom do more than that. But all this is true only if the number of tactical voters remains small. If a voter suspects that there is to be a great deal of tactical voting, his safest strategy will be to vote sincerely. The system is vulnerable to tactical voting in the sense that, if a great many voters indulge in it, the outcome is likely to bear hardly any relation to their true preferences. However convinced we may be of the merits of Borda's criterion for the most representative candidate, there is a danger in adopting his system for parliamentary or local elections when we cannot be confident that sincere voting will be the general rule.

The Borda system is often criticized as allowing what is called 'agenda manipulation'. If it is being used on a committee for deciding between a number of rival proposals, it will be possible for a committee member to secure for some favoured proposal a higher Borda score than it would otherwise obtain by introducing another proposal, very similar to it but evidently inferior to it in a minor degree. In the ideal case, every voter will rank this new proposal just below the one favoured by the committee member, to the latter's considerable advantage. This danger is probably exaggerated even in this case (it is not quite easy to think up a new proposal with these characteristics); but it can be quite disregarded when the system is used for elections. A candidate closely resembling some other candidate, but manifestly inferior in some minor respect, is far from easily found or persuaded to stand.

Whenever there is a likelihood of widespread tactical voting, the Borda system threatens the danger of a completely distorted outcome; and no modification of it, designed to discourage tactical voting, suggests itself. The composite system, on the other hand, provides too little incentive for tactical voting for this to be any grave disadvantage; *its* problem is that of so announcing the results as to avoid charges of unfairness by disappointed voters—a problem to which a solution was offered above. We cannot claim to have arrived at a *perfect* solution to question (1B), as applied to single-member constituencies, whether Condorcet's or Borda's criterion for the most representative single candidate is taken to be the sounder. It is very likely that the problem which is the best electoral system does not admit of a wholly ideal solution, at least in the absence of an ideal electorate.

Nevertheless, none of the systems usually canvassed can be relied on to result in most instances in the election of the candidate who will best represent a single-member constituency. It therefore appears that the Borda system, the modified comparison system, and the composite system vie for being the best that can be devised for the purpose. I am not asking readers to accept this conclusion: my sole purpose has been to persuade them to set about the problem in what, I feel assured, is the only rational way. Some readers may remain unconvinced that the criteria of Condorcet and Borda are the only reasonable ones for picking the most representative single candidate on the basis of voters' preferences. If so, and if they decide that it is right for constituencies to elect only a single MP, their task is first to formulate a criterion that contents them better, and then to devise an electoral system that will normally lead to the election of the candidate who satisfies it when all vote sincerely.

Other readers may agree with me that there is no other plausible criterion, but have an idea how to devise a better electoral system based on whichever criterion they favour. If so, that is all to the good: my wish has been, not to persuade readers of my views, but only to convince them of the right way to go about forming their own.

CHAPTER 9

The Alternative Vote

W HAT in Britain is usually called 'the Alternative Vote' is a system for electing to single-member constituencies. In Australia it is called 'preferential voting'; but in this book we may refer to it by the abbreviation AV. It is an adaptation for a single ballot of an elimination system in which successive ballots are held, each requiring the electors to vote for just one candidate. If, in the first ballot, no candidate secures an absolute majority, the candidate obtaining the fewest votes is eliminated, and a second ballot held between the remainder. If still no candidate secures an absolute majority, the candidate obtaining the fewest votes in this ballot is now eliminated, and a third ballot is held; the ballots continue in this way until some candidate does obtain an absolute majority of the votes, when he is declared elected.

Under AV, all takes place in a single ballot, in which the voters rank as many of the candidates as they choose in order of preference. The tellers calculate the votes in stages. At the first stage, they allot votes to the candidates according to the voters' first choices only (those they rank highest). If any candidate has an absolute majority, he is declared elected. If not, the candidate with the lowest total is eliminated. The votes of those who ranked him highest are then redistributed to the second choices of the voters, save for those ballot-papers on which only one candidate was given a ranking, which are set aside. At this second stage, the totals of votes assigned after the redistribution to the remaining candidates are calculated: if any candidate has more than half of the votes now shared between the uneliminated candidates, he is declared elected. If not, the process is repeated through as many stages as are necessary. At each stage, the candidate with the lowest total is eliminated, and each of the ballot-papers that had been assigned to him is redistributed to the next candidate, if any, on the voter's list who has not yet been eliminated; a ballot-paper that cannot be thus redistributed is set aside.

AV is an improvement on the multiple-ballot system because, in the latter, there is nothing to prevent a voter, for tactical advantage, voting inconsistently in successive ballots; AV thus reduces the opportunity for tactical voting. AV is a distinct improvement upon the plurality system, but, for all that, it is not a particularly good system; it is markedly inferior to the composite score system discussed in the preceding chapter. It may also be regarded as a simplification, for single-member constituencies, of the system known in Britain as the Single Transferable Vote (STV); and this provides the principal reason for studying it. STV is a system for electing to multi-member constituencies, which we shall survey in Chapter 11; but since AV, though a much simpler system, has many of the features of STV, it is best to begin by scrutinizing it. STV occupies an extraordinary position among electoral systems, in that it is the object of a cult. A large body of electoral reformers are committed to STV as to a religious faith; the Electoral Reform Society, in particular, is not a neutral body impartially investigating rival systems and the theory of voting in general, but an organization devoted to disseminating propaganda for STV. Over the decades, there has been a great deal of intensive propaganda for it, from that and other sources; the propaganda is sometimes confused and often highly misleading. It is therefore important, for anyone considering how to improve our electoral system, or whether to stick with the one we have, to consider STV very carefully indeed; as remarked, we had best begin with AV.

It is usually contrary to voters' interests for them not to rank all the candidates in order on their ballot-papers. They may well not do so, under the mistaken impression that it would defeat their own interests to allow their votes to go to a candidate whom they do not greatly like; in thinking this way, they fail to consider that what they fear will happen only if all the candidates whom they do like have been eliminated, and that it will serve their interests better for their votes to go to a candidate they do not like much, in order to keep out one they detest.

Failure to rank all the candidates is also generally inimical to the proper functioning of AV. Under the plurality system, a candidate may be elected even if he is what we called a 'Condorcet tail', that is, if each of the other candidates is preferred by a majority to him; this may well happen in 'split opposition' cases. If every voter ranks all the candidates in order of preference on his ballot-paper (or, what comes to the same, all but one), this cannot happen under AV, unless there has been some extremely ill-judged tactical voting: for the candidate who obtains an absolute majority at the final stage of the assessment, and is therefore elected, must be preferred by that majority to all the candidates—of whom there must be at least one—who have not been eliminated previously. But it can happen under AV if the voters fail to rank all the candidates on their ballot-papers, as the following example shows. There are four candidates, **A**, **B**, **C**, and **D**. The table shows the actual preferences of the voters, not how they fill in their ballot-papers; the figure at the head of each column represents the number of voters having the order of preference shown under it.

4,000	1,500	3,000	6,000	2,000	1,500
A	A	B	C	D	D
B	D	D	A	A	B
C	B	A	B	B	A
D	C	C	D	C	C

A is the Condorcet leader, **B** second in the Condorcet ordering, **C** third, and **D** the Condorcet tail. If all 18,000 voters rank on their ballot-papers, in their true order of preference, just the two candidates they regard as best, the votes will be distributed in stages as follows:

	A	B	C	D
First stage	5,500	3,000	6,000	3,500
Second stage	5,500	——	6,000	6,500
Final stage	——	——	6,000	8,000

Thus **D**, who is the Condorcet tail, will in this case be elected. If the voters had each ranked three (or all four) candidates, this could not have occurred; the distribution of the votes would then have gone the same way until the final stage, when, against **D**'s 8,000, **C** would have been allotted 10,000 votes, 4,000 of which had been redistributed from those of **A**'s supporters who ranked **B** second and **C** third, so that **C** would have been elected instead of **D**.

This is not to say that it is always to a voter's advantage to record all his preferences on his ballot-paper. There are certain circumstances in which it is not; an example will be given towards the end of the chapter. We may nevertheless assume, in further examples, that all voters rank all the candidates (or all but one of them) on their ballot-papers.

AV cannot be fully understood until we consider examples in which there are at least four candidates, so that, unless some candidate attains an absolute majority at the first or second stage of the assessment, two candidates will be eliminated before the final stage is reached with only two candidates remaining. For simplicity, however, it is best to start by considering AV with only three candidates. We shall assume throughout that A is regarded as the best candidate by more voters than either of the other two, and **C** by fewer voters than either of the other two. Hence A's supporters must make up more than a third of the electorate; unless some of them vote tactically by not ranking him highest on their ballot-papers, A is therefore immune from elimination at the first stage, since it is impossible that both the other two candidates should be ranked highest by more voters than he.

Advocates of AV (and of STV) concentrate their propaganda on the fact that supporters of the candidate who is ranked highest by the fewest voters, in our case **C**, who will be eliminated at the first stage if all vote sincerely, are relieved under AV of the perplexity that afflicts them under the plurality system. Under the latter, they are in a quandary whether to vote for their favourite candidate, who has little chance of winning, or to vote tactically for one of the other candidates. Under AV, they are not in this dilemma, for they know that, if their candidate *is* eliminated at the first stage, they have done themselves no harm (though no good either) by ranking him highest on their ballot-papers, since their votes will be transferred to the candidate they ranked second.

This is perfectly true; and by hammering away at the advantage of AV for the supporters of such a candidate, its advocates contrive to insinuate that AV offers *no* incentives for tactical voting and therefore places no voters in any dilemma. We know that this cannot be the case: demonstrably, *every* electoral system will sometimes offer an advantage to tactical voters. What the point illustrates is that it is not those who have the strongest incentive under the plurality system to vote tactically who will have the strongest incentive to do so under AV. This is unsurprising: the mechanism of AV is quite different from that of the plurality system, and the opportunities it offers for tactical voting are therefore also quite different.

When there are just the three candidates **A**, **B**, and **C**, it is indeed true that the supporters of **C** have no opportunity for tactical voting. They can do nothing to prevent **C** from being eliminated at the first stage, and they have no incentive to misrepresent their preferences between the other two. It by no means follows that supporters of the other two candidates cannot benefit from tactical voting.

If **A** is a Condorcet leader, he will be elected under AV, and no voter can prevent this, for, being immune to elimination at the first stage, he is bound to defeat at the second stage whichever candidate is not eliminated, since he is preferred by a majority to him. However, the fact to which advocates of AV persistently fail to draw attention is that there are other reasons save the certainty of being eliminated at the first stage why a candidate may be bound to lose. One of these is his being a Condorcet tail.

What will happen if C is a Condorcet leader, as he well may be if he represents a centre party and A and B right-wing and left-wing parties? There are two cases, according as B or A is the Condorcet tail. If B is the Condorcet tail, he is certain to be defeated at the second stage if he is not eliminated at the first. Supporters of C can do nothing to prevent his elimination, while supporters of A have no incentive to do so, since, if C is eliminated, A will win at the second stage. But supporters of B must ask themselves whether, since they will do their candidate no good by ranking him highest, they might not do themselves some good by *not* ranking him highest. Those of them who prefer C to A may vote tactically by ranking C rather than B highest on their ballot-papers; they may thus cause B to be eliminated at the first stage and hence C to win at the second. They are numerous enough to do this, since they, together with C's supporters, form by hypothesis a majority of the electorate.

This case, in which B cannot win, but certain of his supporters have an incentive to vote tactically in favour of C, is an analogue of the second case under the plurality system considered in Chapter 5. In that case, the candidate who would come second under sincere voting nevertheless stood no chance of winning; but, if a sufficient number of his supporters threw their votes to the candidate who would come last under sincere voting, they would secure his election, which they preferred to that of the superficially most popular candidate.

If C is a Condorcet leader, A may be a Condorcet tail. This may happen in a 'split opposition' case; A is then certain to be defeated at the second stage. In this case, no supporter of B has an incentive to prevent C's elimination at the first stage, since, if he is eliminated, B will win. Likewise, supporters of A who prefer B to C may well vote sincerely and let things take their course. But those of them who prefer C to B are differently placed. They cannot save A; but, if they can cause either B or A to be eliminated instead of C, C will win the election. They may be sufficiently numerous to do this by ranking C highest on their ballot-papers in place of A; and this is quite likely, since, as before, voters who prefer C to B are in a majority. It is of no use to argue that supporters of A are unlikely to care whether B or C wins. Supporters of C are presumed to care whether A or B wins: if they did not, they would have no incentive to vote tactically under the plurality system. Under that system, it is frequently the supporters of the superficially least popular candidate who must think whether to vote tactically; under AV, it may be the supporters of the superficially most popular candidate who must do so.

These examples show the pattern of tactical voting under AV. With only three candidates, the outcome depends entirely on which of the candidates is eliminated at the first stage. Supporters of a candidate who is doomed to be defeated, being, in these examples, a Condorcet tail, may obtain a result they prefer by ranking one of the other two candidates highest on their ballot-papers, thus making sure that a different candidate is eliminated from the one who would have been under sincere voting.

Before we consider what will happen if **B** is the Condorcet leader, let us examine a case in which the majorities are cyclic. Suppose that **A** is preferred by a majority to **B**, **B** to **C**, and **C** to **A**. In this case, **B** cannot win, though not because he is a Condorcet tail, but for a different reason: if he is not eliminated at the first stage, he will be defeated at the second stage by **A**. Hence, as in the case in which **C** was the Condorcet leader and **B** the Condorcet tail, supporters of **B** who prefer **C** to **A** will do well to rank **C** highest on their ballot-papers; with **C**'s supporters, they will again form a majority, and therefore stand a good chance of success, securing the elimination of **B** at the first stage and the victory of **C** at the second.

How, then, will it be if **B** is the Condorcet leader? If *his* supporters amount to more than a third of the electorate, he is immune from elimination at the first stage and is therefore assured of victory. Suppose, then, that his supporters are fewer in number than a third of the electorate. They have no incentive to prevent **C**'s elimination. If **A** is the Condorcet tail, those of his supporters who prefer **C** to **B** may vote tactically by ranking **C** highest on their ballot-papers, so perhaps securing the elimination of **B** and the victory of **C**. If there are too many of them, they may possibly bring about the elimination of **A**, in which case **B** will still win; but they will at least be no worse off than if they had voted sincerely. Moreover, since a majority prefers **B** to **C**, they may be thwarted by counter-tactics on the part of those of **A**'s supporters who, being part of that majority, rank **B** highest on their ballot-papers. **B**'s chances of election are quite high, but they depend in part on whether any electors vote tactically, and, if so, which ones.

We now come to the most interesting and surprising cases. Suppose that **B** is the Condorcet leader, but with the support of less than a third of the electorate, and that **C** is the Condorcet tail. **C**'s supporters can do nothing to affect the outcome, and **B**'s have no incentive to. However, **A**'s only chance of success is that **B** should be eliminated at the first stage. Hence, if some of those of **A**'s supporters who prefer **C** to **B** vote tactically by ranking **C** highest on their ballot-papers, they may bring about the elimination of **B**, in which case **A** may well win. If too many of them adopt this tactic, they will not by this means succeed in getting **A** elected, however, since they have misrepresented themselves as preferring **C** to **A**. As a result, **C** may after all defeat **A** at the second stage; but such an outcome is preferable to them than the victory of **B**. (Under the system with successive ballots, they would have been able to switch their preference to **A** in the second ballot.)

This time, it is not the supporters of a candidate doomed to defeat who have voted tactically to secure the election of the candidate of their second choice. It is, rather, the supporters of one who will lose under sincere voting who have voted tactically to secure *his* election, or, at worst, that of the candidate of their second choice. The possibility is so surprising that it is worth giving a concrete example to demonstrate that it can really occur. The following example will serve the purpose, the columns showing the true preference scales of the voters, and the figures at the head of each column the number of voters with that preference scale:

16,000	2,000	9,000	5,000	4,000	9,000
A	A	B	B	C	C
B	C	A	C	A	B
C	B	C	A	B	A

Here, if all vote sincerely, A will obtain 18,000 votes at the first stage, B 14,000, and C 13,000: C will therefore be eliminated, with 4,000 of his votes going to A and 9,000 to B, who will be elected with 23,000 second-stage votes to A's 22,000. If the 2,000 of A's supporters who prefer C to B vote tactically, however, ranking the candidates in the order C, A, B, then, provided that the remaining voters continue to vote sincerely, A will receive 16,000 first-stage votes, B 14,000, and C 15,000. In this case, therefore, B will be eliminated, 9,000 of his votes being redistributed to A and 5,000 to C; A will thereupon be elected, with 25,000 second-stage votes to C's 20,000. By *not* listing A first, the 2,000 tactical voters have brought about his victory.

This phenomenon is technically known as 'non-monotonicity'. One would naturally expect that, the greater the number of voters who rank a given candidate highest, the greater the chance that candidate will have of winning, or, at least, that by ranking a candidate highest, no voters will diminish his chances. But the example shows that this is not the case under AV. If the 2,000 voters had ranked A highest, they would, by bringing about the elimination of C, have destroyed A's chances of winning. The advocates of AV and of STV have been insistent that no voter can diminish the chances of the candidate they rank highest on their ballot-paper by their choice of the one they rank second; some have even suggested that this encouragement should be printed on the ballot-papers. But none has proposed adding the warning, 'But in some cases you may harm a candidate's chances by ranking him highest.'

Again, the tactics of the 2,000 voters are vulnerable to counter-tactics. Supporters of A who prefer B to C might rank B highest on their ballot-papers; but such a counter-tactic is pointless unless the 2,000 are suspected of tactical voting, and too dangerous for anyone to risk if they are: it may result in the elimination of A at the first stage, when he might have won had these counter-tacticians let well alone. However, C's supporters may engage in counter-tactics too. Unless they think that tactical voting by supporters of A may lead to C's winning, they have no incentive to remain loyal to him. If those who rank the candidates in the order C, B, A all rank B highest on their ballot-papers, they will bring about the election of B outright at the first stage, since, taken together with B's supporters, they form a majority; if, in the above example, 1,000 of them so vote, they will ensure the elimination of C and hence the victory of B.

The phenomenon of non-monotonicity may also occur in the one type of case we have not yet examined, that in which there is a cycle running in the other direction: A is preferred by a majority to C, C to B, and B to A. In such a case, C cannot win: if he is not eliminated at the first stage, he will be defeated at the second stage by A. C's supporters can do nothing about this situation: they can only vote sincerely and hope for the best. B's supporters must hope that voting is sincere; if it is, their candidate will win. But A's supporters can do something. As in the preceding example, **A**'s only chance of winning lies in **B**'s being eliminated at the first stage. If, therefore, all or some of those supporters of **A** who prefer **C** to **B** rank **C** highest on their ballot-papers, they may succeed in getting **B** eliminated at the first stage. They have a good chance, since a majority of the electorate prefers **C** to **B**. If they have deserted **A** in such numbers as to have caused *him* to be eliminated, **C** will win; but they will still have obtained a result they preferred to the election of **B**, which would have occurred had there been no tactical voting. By luck or planning, they may judge the matter sufficiently well by having enough of them to vote for **C** to save him from elimination, but not enough to cause **A** to be eliminated or to overturn his majority over **C** at the second stage.

We may obtain an example of this by slightly modifying the preceding example. Suppose that there are only 8,000 voters whose true ranking of the candidates is in the order **A**, **B**, **C**, and 10,000 whose true ranking is in the order **A**, **C**, **B**, as in the table below:

8,000	10,000	9,000	5,000	4,000	9,000
A	A	B	B	C	C
B	C	A	C	A	B
C	B	C	A	B	A

If more than 1,000 but fewer than 4,000 of the 10,000 whose preference scale is **A**, **C**, **B** vote tactically by ranking **C** highest on their ballot-papers, everyone else voting sincerely, **B** will be eliminated at the first stage and **A** elected at the second, having had 9,000 votes redistributed from **B**, while **C** receives 5,000. If, however, more than 4,000 adopt these tactics, **A** will be eliminated at the first stage and **C** elected at the second. On the other hand, if 2,000 of those with the preference scale **A, C, B** rank **C** highest on their ballot-papers, while 4,000 of those with the preference scale **C, B, A** counter by ranking **B** highest, **C** will be eliminated and **B** will be elected.

It is thus misleading to suggest that supporters of **C** can always safely put him at the head of their lists when he is certain, or very likely, not to be elected. It depends *why* he is certain not to be elected. If it is because he is certain to be eliminated at the first stage, then indeed they will do themselves no harm by putting him at the head of their lists. But if it is because he will be defeated at the second stage if not eliminated at the first, and if there is a danger of tactical voting by others to bring about the election of the candidate lowest in the order of preference of certain of **C**'s supporters, then those supporters will after all have an incentive for voting tactically by putting at the head of their lists the candidate they rank second. They are then in a position very similar to that in which they find themselves under the plurality system, when, **C** having little or no chance of being elected, it will be advantageous for them to vote for **B** if they prefer him to **A**. The propagandists for AV are adept at insinuating that this cannot occur; they do this by fallaciously suggesting that a candidate is doomed to failure *only* when he is certain to be eliminated.

Supporters of AV and STV are particularly annoyed at the charge of non-monotonicity, especially in view of the fact that the Plant Committee, which reported on electoral reform to the British Labour Party, rejected STV on just this score. They cannot deny that these systems are nonmonotonic; they have recourse to claiming the phenomenon to be of exceedingly rare occurrence.* Doubtless non-monotonicity is not the principal demerit of these electoral systems; but it should not be brushed aside. A voter is entitled to be *certain* that, by ranking a candidate highest, he is not harming his chances. The fact that he cannot be certain of this under AV is undoubtedly a grave defect of the system.

AV has been looked at in such detail in this chapter because it is not well understood. Its characteristics become more apparent when there are five or six candidates; but there is no space to survey the more complicated situations that arise even when there are four. All examples involving tactical voting can be interpreted in a different way, namely as illustrating the effects, under sincere voting, of a change of mind on the part of a few voters: what earlier were taken as tactical votes will, under this interpretation, be understood as sincere votes after the preference scales of the voters concerned have changed just before the election actually takes place. It will be found instructive to review the examples given in this chapter in this new light. For the case when there are four candidates, we may content ourselves with a single example, interpreted in just this way. Suppose that the candidates are **A**, **B**, **C**, and **D**. A week before the election is held, the preferences of the 20,500 electors who in the event actually vote are follows:

* Thus, in an article in the journal *representation*, Crispin Allard makes the surely ludicrous underestimate that, under STV, it will occur only in .028% of cases. Only a mass of empirical data could settle the question, since preferences are not distributed randomly; but a rough calculation suggests that, with three candidates under AV, 2% would be a conservative estimate.

1,000	1,000	4,000	3,000	1,000	3,000	1,500	6,000
A	A	A	B	B	C	C	D
B	C	D	C	D	A	D	A
C	B	B	A	A	D	A	B
D	D	C	D	C	B	B	C

If the election had been held at this point, and all voters had ranked the candidates on their ballot-papers in their true order of preference, the votes would have been allotted and redistributed as follows:

	A	B	C	D
First stage	6,000	4,000	4,500	6,000
Second stage	6,000	——	7,500	7,000
Third stage	——	——	9,500	11,000

D would have won, although A was the Condorcet leader. Suppose, however, that, before the election takes place, A makes a widely publicized speech that displeases the 1,000 voters who rank the candidates in the order A, B, C, D; it may be also that B makes one that pleases them. As a result, they change their minds: they now rank B higher than A, their new order of preference thus being B, A, C, D. When the election is held, none of the other voters has changed his mind; all vote sincerely according to their current preferences, and the result is:

	A	B	C	D
First stage	5,000	5,000	4,500	6,000
Second stage	8,000	5,000	——	7,500
Third stage	12,000	——	——	8,500

The effect of the change of mind by the 1,000 voters has thus been the election of **A** in place of the candidate **D** whom they liked least.

It is not especially surprising that a change of mind by less than 5 per cent of the electorate should have a drastic effect upon the outcome: what shows the arbitrariness and instability of AV is the nature of the effect. The 1,000 voters think no worse of **D** than they did before: they always thought him the worst of the four candidates. They think better of **B** than they did, but he does not benefit. They think less well of **A** than they originally did, yet their change of mind greatly benefits him: he is elected, where before he would have been eliminated at the second stage, giving the victory to **D**. **D** is penalized and **A** rewarded simply because a small number of voters have decided that they do not approve of **A** as much as they originally thought they did. The example vividly illustrates how erratically AV may work.

AV is erratic because, at later stages of the assessment process, it gives the same weight to some voters' second, third, or (when there are more than four candidates) fourth choices as it gives to other voters' first choices, while never giving any weight at all to some voters' second or later choices, according to the accidents of which candidates get eliminated and in what order. In particular, it gives no weight to the second or later choices of the supporters of a candidate who survives until the final stage, only then to be defeated. Thus if, in the foregoing example, there had been no change of mind on the part of the 1,000 voters who originally supported **A**, **D** would have beaten **C** at the final stage with 6,000 first-choice votes and 5,000 second-choice ones, as against C's 4,500 first-choice votes, 4,000 second-choice, and 1,000 third-choice ones. As things in fact fell out, A beat D at the final stage with 5,000 first-choice votes, 4,000 second-choice, and 3,000 third-choice ones, as against D's 6,000 first-choice votes and 2,500 second-choice ones.

It was remarked early in this chapter that it is usually to the advantage of a voter to number all the candidates on his ballot-paper in order of preference, but that it is not always so. Here is an example with five candidates to illustrate its sometimes being to certain voters' disadvantage. The preference scales of the voters are as follows, the figures at the head of each column indicating thousands of voters:

14	12	10	1	3	2	1
A	B	C	D	D	E	E
E	E	B	C	E	D	B
B	A	E	B	C	C	C
C	C	A	E	B	B	D
D	D	D	A	A	A	A

If all vote sincerely, and rank all five candidates in order of preference, the assessment process will run as follows:

A	B	C	D	E
14	12	10	4	3
14	13	10	6	—
14	13	16	—	—
26	—	17	—	—

A will be elected, with 26,000 votes to C's 17,000, though thought to be the worst candidate by 7,000 of the voters. If, however, none of those whose first choice was either D or E had assigned numbers to any but those they ranked as

[106]

their two most favoured candidates, the assessment process would have run thus:

A	B	C	D	E
14	12	10	4	3
14	13	10	6	—
14	13	11	—	—
14	23	—	—	—

In this case **B** would have been elected, with 23,000 votes to **A**'s 14,000, a result preferred by all of the 7,000 voters concerned. This would have happened because, when **D** was eliminated, only 1,000 votes would have been transferred to **C** instead of 6,000, with the result that **C** would have been eliminated at the third stage instead of **B**, with a massive transfer of **C**'s votes to **B**. The appropriate comment is the same as that concerning non-monotonicity. Probably very few voters would be able to tell that they could gain an advantage by not recording their later preferences: but they ought to be entitled to be assured that they could *not* do so.

AV is superior to the plurality system, in that it gives an opportunity for every voter to register all his preferences, and also in that (when all the voters rank all the candidates, which we have just seen is not invariably in their interests) a candidate who is a Condorcet tail cannot be elected, as he well may be (and probably often is) under the plurality system. It is also superior to the two-ballot system used in France. This is a variant on the multiple-ballot elimination system mentioned at the beginning of this chapter, and combines the defects of two systems. If, in elections for the National Assembly, no candidate obtains an absolute majority in the first ballot, all those receiving less than 10 per cent of the total vote are eliminated, unless there was only one candidate with 10 per cent or more, in which case the one receiving the second highest vote stays in; the candidate obtaining the highest number of votes in the second ballot is elected. In presidential elections, all but the two candidates receiving the greatest number of votes are eliminated. On the other hand, AV is inferior to the composite system and (when few indulge in tactical voting) to the Borda system, because it is based on no clear principle. It may easily result in the election of the candidate who is last but one in the Condorcet ordering, being preferred by a majority to only one other candidate. Quite a small number of voters may serve to determine which candidate is eliminated at each stage; this has disproportionate effects on which votes are redistributed and hence on the subsequent course of the assessment process. This is the reason for its erratic character, which makes it impossible to discern anything fair about it.

CHAPTER 10

The Wasted Vote

UNLIKE 'the Alternative Vote', 'the Wasted Vote' is not the name of an electoral system. It is, rather, a phrase whose meaning is highly uncertain, though much in use by advocates of AV and STV.

It was said at the end of Chapter 9 that AV is not based on any clear principle. It might have been fairer to say that it is not based on any clear criterion for the most representative candidate, such as Condorcet's and Borda's criteria. It *is* based on an idea, though that idea is far from being a clear one. The idea is to minimize the number of electors who waste their votes. The aim is therefore to be as fair as possible to the voters; and such an aim is not intrinsically unsound. We saw that it is the object of an electoral system to be fair to the *voters* rather than to the *candidates*. More exactly, the two aims coincide, for the purpose of a constituency election is to select the most *representative* candidate or candidates, not the one or more who are the best by some other standard: hence to be fair to the voters *is* to be fair to the candidates. Yet the extensive discussion of wasted votes is not directed towards identifying the most representative candidates and securing their election, but to the idea of making as many as possible of the electors' votes count by preventing their being wasted; and unfortunately it is never explained in any of that discussion what someone's wasting his vote consists in.

How can what is meant by wasting one's vote be obscure? The thought that he has wasted his vote comes so easily to a remorseful elector. Suppose Miss Jones voted, under the plurality system, for the candidate C, who came third in the poll, while A, whom she detested, won, though without an absolute majority, closely followed by B, whom she much preferred to A. If only she and others of her mind had voted for B, they might have defeated A: in voting for C, they wasted their votes.

In such a case, there is indeed no unclarity about the notion. What Miss Jones means is that to her and others like her there was open a way of voting which would, had they adopted it, have produced an outcome they all greatly preferred to the actual one. But this explanation is not general enough for the purpose to which the concept of the wasted vote is put by propagandists for AV and STV. Miss Jones is comparing the actual outcome with that which she and her friends would have obtained *under the plurality system* if they had voted a different way, provided that everyone else had voted as before. But the propagandists wish to compare *different* electoral systems: they are recommending AV because it will involve fewer wasted votes than the plurality system. We therefore need to know, not merely what it is to waste one's vote under the plurality system, but what it is to waste one's vote under *any* given system.

Well, will not the explanation already suggested serve the purpose? According to this, one has wasted one's vote, under any particular electoral system, if, by voting differently, one could, *under that same system*, have obtained an outome one preferred. This tallies with the common notion of waste: I waste my time if I have something better to do with it, and I waste my money if I have something more worth while to spend it on. As it stands, the definition will make a wasted vote very rare indeed, since it seldom happens that just one elector, by voting differently, could have produced a different outcome. We may therefore emend it as follows: one has wasted one's vote, under a particular electoral system, if all those with the same preferences between the candidates as oneself could, by voting differently under that same system, have obtained an outome they all preferred.

Suppose that **B** would have won, under the plurality system, if Miss Jones and those who thought like her had voted for him instead of **C**; then, by the foregoing definition, Miss Jones would have wasted her vote. If AV had been in force, they would have ranked **C** highest and **B** second. **C** would very probably have been eliminated, and their votes have been transferred to **B**, who would almost certainly have won. Miss Jones would *not* then have wasted her vote. It would have done her no good to rank **B** highest, and there was no way in which she could have prevented **C**'s elimination. AV would have saved her from wasting her vote. That is the general message advocates of AV wish to transmit: AV saves wasted votes!

It is on cases like this—call it case (1)—that the propaganda for AV is intended to make us concentrate our attention. But suppose now that, under AV, when **C** had been eliminated, **A**, despite the transfer of votes, defeated **B**: a sufficient number of the ballot-papers ranking **C** highest had been transferred to **A**. Miss Jones has still not wasted her vote under AV: but does the supposition entail that she would *not* have wasted her vote under the plurality system if she had voted for **C**? It does not. For it may be that if she and all the others of **C**'s supporters who preferred **B** to **A** had voted for **B**, **B** would have won. She would then still have wasted her vote, by our definition, under the plurality system; she would not have wasted it under AV, but that would have been no great consolation to her, because the candidate she hated would still have won. She might, rather, regret the substitution of AV for the plurality system, which would have given her and like-minded people an opportunity to get **B** elected, if only they had taken it. Let us call this case (2).

It may be objected that in case (2) it may well be that **A** *ought* to have won. He may be the Condorcet leader, or, if majorities are cyclic, have the highest Borda count. This is irrelevant. We are not now considering which system is most likely to bring about the election of the candidate who, by one or other criterion, is the most representative: we are considering the claim selected by the advocates of AV themselves as the most telling advantage of the system, that it saves wasted votes.

A quite different objection may be made. This is that, in case (2), a majority of electors must prefer **A** to **B**, since it was assumed that **A** would beat **B** under AV when **C** had been eliminated. It follows that if, under the plurality system, supporters of **C** had voted tactically for **A**, there would have been a sufficient number of them to give **A** an absolute majority, and certainly to thwart tactical voting in favour of **B**. That is perfectly true. It does not, however, show that

Miss Jones and others of the same mind did not waste their votes. The definition was that one has wasted one's vote, under a particular electoral system, if all those with the same preferences between the candidates as oneself could, by voting differently under that same system, have obtained an outome they all preferred. The tacit assumption behind this definition was that, when those in question voted differently to obtain an outcome they preferred, everyone else would vote as before. If we so understand the definition, then in case (2) Miss Jones and her fellows *have* wasted their votes.

But is the definition, so understood, the right one? It has the consequence that one cannot always tell, just from knowing the preferences of all the voters, which of them will be wasting their votes if they vote in a particular way. In case (2), under the plurality system, if everyone votes sincerely, those of C's supporters who, like Miss Jones, prefer B to A will have wasted their votes, since, by voting for B, they could have got him elected, given that everyone else had continued to vote sincerely. Those of C's supporters who preferred A to B would not have wasted their votes, on the other hand, since they could not have obtained an outcome that they preferred. But if the former group of C's supporters had voted tactically for B, the rest voting sincerely, then those who preferred A to B *would* have wasted their votes, since, by voting tactically for A, they would have obtained an outcome that they preferred. The notion of the wasted vote now seems less clear than it did at first.

Should we emend our definition to require, for the voters in a given set to be said to have wasted their votes, that, if they had voted differently, they could have made *certain* of getting an outcome that they preferred, however the other electors voted? On this understanding, Miss Jones and her fellows did not waste their votes by voting for C in case (2), because they had no way to make certain of obtaining an outcome they preferred to the election of A. It still remains, however, that we cannot say whether or not those of C's supporters who preferred A to B wasted their votes without knowing how Miss Jones and her fellows voted. This is because the definition requires us to compare the outcome obtained by voting in some different way with the *actual* outcome. If everyone had voted sincerely, A would have been elected; those of C's supporters who preferred A to B could not then have obtained an outcome that they preferred, let alone have made certain of doing so, by voting in any other way, and so did not waste their votes on our current understanding of the notion. But if Miss Jones and her fellows had voted tactically for B, the rest voting sincerely, B would have won the election; in that case, those of C's supporters who preferred A to B could have made certain of an outcome they preferred by voting tactically for A, and so did waste their votes by casting them for C. We are still in difficulties to explain what we mean by saying that someone has wasted his vote.

Let us consider a different case. We laid it down that, under the plurality system, a candidate should be regarded as having no chance of election if the number of electors who preferred him to the candidate having the greatest number of supporters was less than the number of those supporters. Obviously, if, when voting between our three candidates is sincere, A wins the election, B comes second, and C bottom of the poll, it may well be that C had, by this criterion, no chance of winning, but that B would have won if there had been tactical voting in his favour. We have also noted the neglected possibility that **B** may have had no chance of winning, but that tactical voting by *his* supporters would have ensured **C**'s victory. But it is also possible that *either* could have occurred: that if sufficiently many of **C**'s supporters had voted tactically for **B**, they could have ensured the election of **B**, *but also*, that if sufficiently many of **B**'s supporters had voted tactically for **C**, they could have ensured the election of **C**. It is here being assumed that in either case the tactical voters would have obtained an outcome they preferred to the election of **A**; the assumption is likely in instances of a 'split opposition'. We may call this case (3).

Of which set of voters, if any, are we to say in case (3) that they wasted their votes? If all voted sincerely, those supporters of **C** who preferred **B** to **A** could, by voting differently, have made certain of **B**'s election; but, equally, those supporters of **B** who preferred **C** to **A** could, by voting differently, have made certain of **C**'s election. In this case, the concept of the wasted vote has utterly broken down.

It is true enough that AV solves the problem of the split opposition. When a majority prefers **B** to **A**, and a majority prefers **C** to **A** too, **A** cannot be elected under AV. The opponents of **A** are no longer in a quandary whether to vote for **B** or for **C**: they can all vote sincerely, content that one or other of the two will defeat **A** in the end. Our present concern is not with the claim that AV leaves voters less often in a quandary than does the plurality system. The claim is probably true, though our review of tactical voting under AV showed that it too can create quandaries. But our present concern is with the notion of wasting one's vote; and this has stood up very badly under scrutiny.

Our survey of AV disclosed various cases in which, under it, some set of electors would be said by any standard to have wasted their votes. Suppose that, if C were eliminated, A would defeat B, but, if B were eliminated, C would defeat A; A is immune to elimination at the first stage. B is therefore doomed to defeat. Those of his supporters who prefer C to A accordingly waste their votes by ranking B highest on their ballot-papers, thus bringing about C's elimination and A's election; if they rank C highest, C's own supporters remaining staunch, C will be elected.

There are also cases under AV in which the concept of the wasted vote breaks down. An instance is a case like that discussed towards the end of the last chapter. B is the Condorcet leader, and C the Condorcet tail; if all vote sincerely, C will be eliminated and B elected. If some of A's supporters who prefer C to B vote tactically by ranking C highest, they may cause B to be eliminated and A to be elected. If all vote sincerely, which of them have wasted their votes? It is difficult to say that any of A's supporters have done so, given that a large number must remain faithful to him if he is not to be eliminated at the first stage. Those supporters of C who preferred B to A could have made sure that B was not eliminated by ranking him highest; they had no real motive to rank C highest, given that, being the Condorcet tail, he could not win. As things are, however, they would have gained no advantage by doing so, since B was in the event elected. In a situation such as this, it becomes quite pointless to talk of wasted votes; the concept is too coarse to be of any use.

When advocates of AV or of STV speak of people wasting their votes under the plurality system, they mean it in a sense similar to that of our first definition, though they are never very precise about their meaning. But when they apply the notion to AV or STV, they use it in a wholly different sense. If someone's vote is twice transferred, say, and eventually goes to elect the candidate of his third or fourth choice, they describe it as not having been wasted; it helped to make a difference to the outcome, and so it cannot have been wasted. The only wasted votes will be those which were never transferred to a candidate who was eventually elected. This confers quite a different meaning on 'wasting one's vote': in comparing votes under the plurality system which advocates of AV count as not having been wasted with those under AV that they count as not having been wasted, they are not comparing like with like.

If we apply the notion of wasting one's vote to the plurality system in the same way as advocates of AV or STV apply it to those systems, everyone must count as wasting his vote who does not vote for the winning candidate. It is then easy to show that, in view of their redistributions of votes, AV and STV will involve fewer wasted votes than the plurality system. But, when wasted votes are under discussion, it is necessary to ask what makes wasting one's vote a bad thing. If, under the plurality system, an elector realizes that, if he had voted differently, he might have helped a candidate that he preferred to win, he will regret the way he voted. But, given the candidate who did win, the fact that he did not contribute to his victory is no *additional* cause of regret; and, if he could have done nothing to prevent that victory, he will have no regrets about the way he voted. He may, of course, wish that a different electoral system had been in force; but surely not for the reason, in itself, that his own vote might have contributed to the result, but because there would have been a fairer outcome or one that he would have preferred.

Equally, it is no great consolation in itself for a voter under AV to reflect that his vote went to elect the candidate of his third choice. It will be some consolation to think that his vote helped to elect a candidate whom he preferred to the one who would have been elected had he never visited the polling station; but this will be strongly offset if he realizes that he could have helped to bring about an even better result if he had voted another way. The consolation will be negligible if he realizes that the candidate he favoured was the most representative and would have been elected under some fairer system. The consolation will be non-existent if, as may happen under AV, it proves that a candidate he much preferred to the one who was in fact elected would have won if he had not voted at all.

The concept of the wasted vote is thoroughly confused, and wholly unhelpful in thinking about electoral systems. What *is* significant is the degree of incentive to tactical voting which an electoral system offers. This is difficult to quantify, because it depends on so many different factors. Given a particular system and a particular distribution of preferences among the electors, we can of course tell how many electors would profit by voting tactically, given that all others voted sincerely. A more sophisticated question would be how many electors would be voting tactically in an *equilibrium* situation. An equilibrium situation consists in a complete record of how each elector votes, in which no set of electors could, by voting differently, obtain a result that they all preferred, the remaining electors voting as before.

The answer to either question would be entirely theoretical, however. Whether any electors will vote tactically will depend on how likely they are to guess how other electors will vote, and their estimates of the risk that tactical voting will make the result worse for them rather than better. Moreover, the general incentive to tactical voting offered by the given electoral system will depend on the probability that electors will vote tactically under all other distributions of preferences, and on how likely it is that preferences will be distributed in the various different ways; these probabilities could be reliably assessed only after a massive empirical investigation. In the absence of a convincing formal means of measuring each electoral system's vulnerability to tactical voting, it is therefore best to rely on informal considerations. Under some electoral systems, such as the plurality system, it will often be obvious how to vote tactically with little risk, though not always: supporters of the candidate likely to come third under sincere voting will often see the advantage of voting for the one likely to come second, but, as we saw, supporters of the candidate likely to come second will seldom realize the advantage of voting for the one likely to come third. Under some other systems, successful tactical voting will depend on thorough knowledge of other voters' intentions: to be aware of the effect under AV of causing one candidate to be eliminated instead of another requires a good knowledge of the relative preferences of the electorate between pairs of candidates. Such facts may be noted, and may legitimately influence our choice of electoral system, without the need for any precise measure of the incentive to tactical voting given by any arbitrary system. Appeal to the muddled notion of the wasted vote, by contrast, should be entirely eschewed in any discussion of the topic.

CHAPTER 11

Multi–Member Constituencies

UNDER virtually any reasonable electoral system, the election of Members of Parliament from large constituencies returning from two to six members will result in a more representative selection of MPs than their election from small constituencies returning only one member each. Suppose that, at a given time, 42 per cent of the electorate in five adjacent single-member British constituencies taken together favour the Conservatives, while 39 per cent favour Labour, and the remaining 19 per cent the Liberal Democrats. Then, if the support for Labour is concentrated in one of the five constituencies, they would, under the plurality system, together return four Conservative MPs and one Labour one. If the Liberal Democrat voters predominantly favoured the Labour Party over the Conservatives, AV might result in the election of five Labour MPs. Plainly, such results are inequitable. If the five constituencies were amalgamated into one returning five MPs, probably two Conservative, one Liberal Democrat, and two Labour candidates would be elected.

Multi-member constituencies are thus naturally favoured

by those concerned with making Parliament more representative. They are particularly favoured by those anxious to achieve something approaching proportional representation, but reluctant to abandon the constituency principle whereby Parliament (or its lower House) is exclusively composed of constituency representatives. If the dual-vote device is found acceptable, a desire to achieve PR ceases to be so strong a motive for favouring multi-member constituencies. Their claim is then, rather, that they achieve better *local* representation. A citizen may prefer to have an MP who represents a small constituency that sends only one member to Parliament, and who is therefore more likely to be sympathetic to the relatively uniform needs and interests of that small area, despite the elector's disapproval of the MP's politics. But it can easily work the other way. A voter in a constituency that sends several MPs to Westminster has all of them to choose from when he needs an MP to help him or when he wants to urge a political cause, and may well feel more hopeful or more comfortable with a politician with whose views he is in sympathy. The point is debatable; different individuals will feel differently about it. What is not debatable is that multi-member constituencies can achieve representation for local minorities, too small on a national scale to attain it through the workings of PR applied nationally.

The outcome of an election in a multi-member constituency is, of course, the return to Parliament of not one, but several, of the candidates, normally from three to five. It could be argued, therefore, that the ideal system would be to require the voters to rank, in order of preference, as many of the possible total outcomes as they chose, such outcomes consisting of a choice of as many candidates as there were seats to be filled. The winning outcome could then be determined by allotting Borda scores to the possible outcomes (treating any omitted from a voter's ballot-paper as if bracketed equal below all those he had ranked). By this means, a voter would be given the opportunity to express conditional wishes, such as that he thought each of two candidates highly worthy of election, but that he did not wish to see both elected. This method, however, is quite impracticable. With only three seats to be filled, and only nine candidates standing for them, there would be 84 possible outcomes, all, presumably, to be listed on the ballot-paper; voters would find it tedious to be asked to rank even fifteen of them.

If voters are asked to rank *candidates* in order of preference, Borda scores could of course be calculated for them, rather than for possible total outcomes; some information would be lost, and some opportunity denied to voters for expressing their wishes, but we should be in the realm of practical possibility, especially if tellers were allowed to use calculators. It would be pointless to determine whether any candidate was a Condorcet leader, what the Condorcet ranking of the candidates was (if such a ranking could be assigned to them) or what their Copeland scores were: the notion of a majority has no significant role to play in deciding which three or more candidates are severally the most representative. By contrast, the Borda score of a candidate is an index of his general popularity or acceptability. A candidate's having a high level of general popularity should surely count as one criterion for his being a good representative of a multi-member constituency; for the purpose of an election in a multi-member constituency is to identify

those candidates who best represent the constituency electorate at large. General popularity is not the only criterion
for a candidate's deserving to be elected, however. The great
merit of large constituencies returning several Members of
Parliament is that by means of them we can secure representation for *minorities*. It is his being qualified to represent
a sufficiently large minority that constitutes the other, and
overriding, criterion of a candidate's right to be elected.

How large is a 'sufficiently large' minority? There can be
no principled answer to this question in general. It is
important that minorities that have, or strongly feel themselves to have, needs and interests distinct from those of the
majority should not lack a voice to make the nation, and the
legislature in particular, aware of those needs and interests.
In some countries—notably in India under British rule—
minorities have been guaranteed representation by means of
reserved seats. In Britain itself seats have never been
reserved for specific sections of the population. The need
for minorities to be represented has indeed sometimes been
acknowledged by the House of Commons; it has been provided for by electoral systems intended to bring this about.
When there are no reserved seats, and minorities have to
identify themselves solely by how they vote, a definite
answer can be given to the question how large they have to
be within any one constituency for an electoral system to be
capable of guaranteeing them representation.

A constituency that returns two Members to Parliament
obviously cannot guarantee representation to all minorities
forming no more than a third of the electorate, since there
might be three of them: the electoral system can at best be
designed to secure representation for any minority forming

more than a third of the electorate, of which there could not be more than two. Similarly, if there are three seats to be filled, the system may be designed to secure representation for any minority forming more than a quarter of the electorate, of which there could not be more than three. If four seats are to be filled, it would be possible to guarantee representation to any minority forming more than a fifth of the electorate, and, if five seats, to any forming more than a sixth. This is the best that any electoral system could do in this regard; since, in a democratic society, it should be a prime aim of an electoral system to secure representation for minorities, we must take these proportions as the sizes of minorities within a local electorate that ought to be represented. For this purpose, a balance must be struck between sizes of constituencies too great for a minority to constitute a sufficient sector of the electorate and those with too few seats for it to attain the required proportion of it; this obviously depends on the geographical distribution of different sections of the population. It may be that a minority too small or too scattered to form this proportion of the electorate in any multi-member constituency ought nevertheless to be represented in the national Parliament. The only remedy is then some system of proportional representation applied at national level by means of additional Members of Parliament. This will be possible only if the minority is represented by some political party of its own. As we shall see, constituency elections may be able to secure representation for minorities not organized by parties: PR, at national level, can take account of them only when they are so organized.

Among systems actually used for elections in multi-member constituencies, we may set aside, as obviously undesirable, those employing party lists. Under these, the voters decide how many candidates of each party are to be elected, but, when they have so decided, it is the party which, by listing its candidates in *its* order of preference, decides which of those candidates will be elected. Of other systems, the limited multiple vote system was used in Britain from 1867 to 1884 for the multi-member constituencies existing in that period, thirteen of them electing to three seats and one to four. Under this system, each voter may place a cross against the names of more than one candidate (two in three-member constituencies, three in four-member constituencies), without ranking them in order: the candidates with the greatest numbers of votes are elected.*

This system has very little merit; the same holds good of all systems requiring electors to cast some fixed number of undifferentiated votes for several candidates. If there are six candidates, there are 720 ways in which an elector might rank them in order of preference; by casting undifferentiated votes for two of them, there being three seats to be filled, an elector will indicate (if he is voting sincerely) only that he has some one out of 48 of these possible preference scales: a great deal of information relevant to which candidates ought to be elected will have been lost. In consequence, the results are often erratic, even when all the electors vote sincerely: it is not difficult to construct examples in which the candidates who would be elected when the voters are restricted to casting two votes would not be elected if they were permitted to cast three. The system puts a high premium on party organization; a party machine

* See Vernon Bogdanor, *The People and the Party System* (Cambridge, 1981), pp. 103–4.

is given a strong incentive for instructing supporters of the party how to cast their votes so as to maximize the number of candidates of that party who will be elected. Nor is it effective in protecting minorities: when three votes are to be cast, a minority must constitute at least two-fifths of the electorate to be sure of getting a representative elected.

A quite different system is usually advocated for use in multi-member constituencies. In Britain and elsewhere it is usually known as STV ('Single Transferable Vote'); in Australia it is called 'Hare-Clark', after the names of early propagandists for it. In Britain, this system is the subject of intensive propaganda, above all by the Electoral Reform Society. It is akin to AV, with which it shares some basic features but which is easy to explain. In use in Ireland and in Malta (and formerly in Northern Ireland), and for the election of the Australian and Nepalese Senates and for the Parliament of Nauru, STV is the most complicated system ever actually employed. As under AV, the voters rank as many candidates as they choose in order of preference; and, also as under AV, the assessment process carried out by the tellers proceeds by stages. The first step is to compute a quota, which any candidate has to attain in order to be elected. The one usually used is called the Droop quota, after its inventor, H. R. Droop, who proposed it in a book of 1881. It depends on the number of seats to be filled and the number of those actually voting. The number of voters is divided by one more than the number of seats to be filled; the quota is the next highest whole number. Thus, if there are 60,000 voters and five seats to be filled, the quota is 10,001; it remains at 10,001 if there are from 60,001 to 60,005 voters, and jumps to 10,002 if the number of voters reaches 60,006. This quota (given that it is to be a whole number) is quite correctly defined, being the smallest whole number such that no more candidates could receive that number of votes than there are seats to be filled. Thus, out of 60,003 votes cast, it would be impossible for more than five candidates to receive 10,001 votes each. It is regarded as an analogue of an absolute majority in an election to a single-member constituency, a majority being any number higher than half the number of votes cast. The quota is thus set as low as possible. This assists the election of candidates favoured by minorities, a feature which we shall see to be the great merit of STV. It will be evident that the way in which the Droop quota is defined is prompted by considerations analogous to those we reviewed in discussing the size of minorities that can expect to be represented.

At the first stage of the assessment process, each candidate is assigned as many votes as there are ballot-papers on which he is ranked highest. At each stage, a candidate is declared elected if, at that stage, he has attained a number of votes equal to or greater than the quota. If no candidate has attained the quota, the candidate who, at the given stage, has the smallest number of votes is eliminated. In preparation for the next stage, all his votes are, if possible, redistributed to other candidates who are still live: a candidate is live if he has not yet been eliminated and has not yet attained the quota. Each of the eliminated candidate's votes is redistributed to the next candidate on the voter's ballot-paper who is still live. If there remains no live candidate who has been ranked by the voter on his ballot-paper, that ballot-paper is set aside and not further considered.

When a candidate attains the quota at any stage, there is

no elimination. Instead, votes are redistributed from the candidate who has attained the quota. They are not redistributed *in toto*, however, but only to the extent of the number of 'surplus' votes, that is to say, the difference between the number of votes assigned to the successful candidate at that stage and the quota (the minimum number of votes he required to be declared elected). Thus, if the quota is 10,002 and a candidate has, at a certain stage, acquired a total of 13,336 votes, entitling him to be declared elected, the surplus will be 3,334 votes to be redistributed. There are various ways of doing this. The only fair way is to redistribute *all* the successful candidate's votes, or rather, all those that are not to be set aside as having no live candidate ranked on the ballot-paper, but at a fractional value. The fraction is given by dividing the surplus by the total number of votes assigned to the successful candidate at that stage. In our example, this will be 3,334 divided by 13,336, that is to say a quarter. Each of the 13,336 votes will then be redistributed to the next live candidate, if any, ranked by the voter on his ballot-paper, but will count only as ¼ of a vote. If any of the votes assigned to the successful candidate to make up his 13,336 votes already has a fractional value, as having been redistributed from some previously successful candidate, its new value will be determined by multiplying both fractions. If, for example, one of the votes to be redistributed from the candidate having 13,336 votes has a fractional value of ⅓, its new value will be ⅓ × ¼, that is, ¹⁄₁₂.

The most accurate way of carrying out the assessment process under STV is to recalculate the quota at each stage. In such a recalculation, the total number of votes originally cast will be replaced by the number of those not yet set aside, but still assignable to some live candidate, whether at their full value or as fractional votes. Likewise, the total number of seats to be filled is replaced by the number remaining to be filled at the given stage. Thus suppose that there are five seats, and 60,003 votes are cast. The quota therefore originally stands at 10,001. At the first stage, no candidate obtains the quota, so the candidate F with the fewest votes, say 4,000, is eliminated. 604 of those who made F their first choice listed no other candidate; their ballot-papers are therefore set aside. The remaining 3,396 votes for F are now redistributed, so that there are now 59,399 votes remaining live. The quota is then recalculated before the next stage. Since none of the five seats has yet been filled, we have to divide 59,399 by 6, giving 9,899 with a remainder of 5: the new quota is therefore 9,900.

Suppose that, at the second stage, a candidate A obtains 9,999 votes, thus attaining the new quota. The surplus is 99: so A's 9,999 votes will be redistributed, as far as possible, at a fractional value of $\frac{1}{101}$. Suppose that, of these, 202 voters listed no candidates other than A and F; 9,797 votes will therefore be redistributed at the fractional value, making the equivalent of a total of 97 votes. This gives the equivalent of 49,497 votes remaining live. Since there are now only four seats remaining to be filled, we must divide this total by 5 to obtain the quota applicable at the next stage: this yields 9,899 with a remainder of 2, so that the quota will again be taken as 9,900.

In practice, this recalculation is very seldom done: it *is* done by the Australian Electoral Commission for elections to the Senate, but much more usually the quota remains what it was at the outset. The assessment process is complete once as many candidates have attained the quota as there are seats to be filled: when this has happened, no other candidate could attain the quota. But when the quota has not been recalculated after each stage of the assessment process, it may happen that a stage is reached at which it is impossible for any remaining live candidate to attain the (unrevised) quota. In this case, once it is clear which candidate or candidates, up to the number of seats remaining to be filled, will have the highest numbers of votes assigned to them, those candidates will be declared elected. Suppose, for example, that one seat remains to be filled, the quota being 10,002. At the final stage, three candidates remain live: **C**, with 5,011 votes, **D** with 3,123, and **E** with 1,694. If **E** were eliminated, and all his votes found to be redistributable to **D**, **D** would still have fewer votes than **C**. Despite the fact that **C** could not attain the quota even if all the votes of the other two candidates were redistributed to him, he is therefore declared elected, without any need to continue the assessment process. If the quota had been recalculated, then, since only one seat remains to be filled, it would come to a majority of the 9,828 votes divided between the three candidates, namely 4,915, and **C** could then be said to have attained it.

The complexity of this description requires an apology to the reader: but it is unavoidable. STV simply *is* complex. It is highly doubtful that many of those who vote under this system could give an accurate account of how it works. It is complicated for the tellers, too (they would be greatly assisted by the use of a computer). Under most electoral systems, the tellers need do nothing but count and add (under the plurality system, they need know nothing more than how to count). Under STV, they must multiply and divide, as well, and handle ungainly fractions (or decimal approximations to them). Whatever merits STV may have, simplicity is not one of them.

If the redistribution of the surplus from a candidate who has attained the quota is carried out in the manner described above—the only fair way of doing it—then, after the first such redistribution, the total of votes assigned to one or more of the candidates is very unlikely to be a whole number. In this case, there was not really any reason for the quota to be a whole number, either. It could just as well have been taken to be, not the smallest whole number greater than the result of dividing the number of voters by one more than the number of seats to be filled, but simply the result of carrying out that division, which will not, in general, be a whole number. If the quota is so understood, a candidate will be declared elected, not as soon as he *attains* the quota, but as soon as the total value of the votes assigned to him *surpasses* the quota, by any margin, however narrow.

As under AV, it is seldom in any voter's interest not to rank all the candidates on his ballot-paper. The thought, 'I do not want my vote used to elect *her*,' referring to a candidate whom the voter greatly dislikes, is a very natural one to have; it should be countered by the thought, 'My vote will have been of some use if it serves to get *her* elected rather than *him*,' apropos of another candidate whom the voter utterly abhors. Unless a voter is genuinely indifferent between those candidates whom he chooses not to rank on his ballot-paper, it can usually do him only harm to have his ballot-paper set aside at some stage as no longer capable of being redistributed.

When the supporters of some political party vote, under STV, along party lines, they will rank all candidates of that party higher than every other candidate, though not necessarily in the same order among themselves. When the voters belonging to some group concur in ranking every member of some set of candidates higher than any candidate not in that set (though not all ranking the candidates in the set in the same order), we may say that the group of voters is giving *solid support* to the set of candidates in question. When there is solid support for certain sets of candidates, the pattern of voting may be described as 'clumped'. STV shows at its best when votes are strongly clumped.

In 1880, all three places in the multi-member constituency of Birmingham were filled by Liberal Party candidates; no Conservative succeeded in getting elected. This was achieved by careful organization on the part of the Liberal Party machine. The election was conducted under the multiple vote system, according to which each voter could nominate two candidates, without indicating a preference between them. The party machine had issued cards to all supporters of the party, instructing them for which two Liberal candidates to vote; by this means, votes were distributed evenly between the three Liberal candidates, enabling all of them to obtain more votes than any of the Conservative candidates. Something similar might be attempted under a system using Borda scores for individual candidates. Alternatively, under such a Borda system, a party unsure of winning any seat might instruct its supporters all to rank a particular candidate highest. Under STV, any such method of rigging the result would be pointless. If the supporters of a party are sufficiently numerous to make sure of getting one candidate of that party elected, then, provided that they do give solid support to the candidates standing on behalf of the party, one such candidate will be elected, regardless of the order in which the party's supporters choose to rank those candidates. Here 'sufficiently numerous' means 'at least equal in number to the quota'; in other words, the party's supporters form a sufficiently large minority in the sense previously explained. Likewise, if the party's supporters are sufficiently numerous to make sure of getting two candidates of the party elected, then, provided that they give solid support to the party's candidates, two such candidates are bound to be elected, however those supporters rank the candidates amongst themselves. In this case, 'sufficiently numerous' means 'at least equal in number to twice the quota'.

Suppose that, in a constituency which is to return four members to Parliament, 90,000 ballot-papers are filled: the quota is then 18,001. If 19,256 voters give solid support to the four candidates standing on behalf of the Radical Party, one of those candidates will be elected, even though no other vote goes to any Radical candidate. For by a stage in the assessment process at which only one Radical candidate remains live, either one of the other three will have attained the quota, or all three will have been eliminated. If all three have been eliminated, all their votes will have been redistributed to the remaining live Radical candidate, who will therefore have collected all the 19,256 votes cast by supporters of the party; he will therefore have attained the quota, and will be declared elected. Again, suppose that there had been 36,115 voters giving solid support to the four

Radical candidates—over twice the quota—though no other vote goes to any Radical candidate. Suppose that, at some stage of the assessment, one of the Radical candidates is declared elected with 19,221 votes. At that stage, 16,894 votes must be divided between the remaining live Radical candidates; but a surplus equivalent to 1,220 votes will be redistributed from the one declared elected, and these will all go to the other Radical candidates who remain live. Thus, in all, by the next stage 18,114 votes will be divided between the remaining live Radical candidates; since this figure exceeds the quota, the foregoing argument shows that one other Radical candidate will eventually attain the quota and be declared elected.

The ability of STV to guarantee representation for sufficiently large minorities, provided that their members, when voting, give solid support to the candidates representative of them, is not confined to minorities defined by their adhesion to particular political parties, or organized in any other way. The minorities are not identified by the system by political labels, but solely by the pattern of their ranking of the candidates on their ballot-papers. A minority not spoken for by any political party can therefore be sure, if it is sufficiently large and sufficiently determined to be represented, of obtaining such representation under STV, provided that it can identify one or more of the candidates whom it would trust to speak on its behalf. This might be a racial or religious minority, or a social or economic group.

The representation of such minorities is a serious matter. The Labour Party recently adopted a clumsy, and, as it proved, illegal, method for increasing the number of women MPs; the length of time it took to get any members of our racial minorities into the House of Commons is a reproach both to our political parties and to our electoral system. Who can point to any member of the House and say with assurance that he speaks on behalf of the unemployed? These are sectors of the population with distinct concerns which, in our representative democracy, go unrepresented; there are no doubt others. Probably few members of these groups would treat their loyalty to the group as overriding their preference for one or another political party. Members of a racial minority cannot be counted on to give solid support to all candidates belonging to that minority, or sympathetic to it, irrespective of party. But in a constituency in which a particular party is strong, those of its supporters who belong to some national minority may be numerous enough to form by themselves what we are calling a sufficiently large minority of the constituency electorate.

A minority giving solid support to a set of candidates may be composed of supporters of some 'single issue', such as penal reform, animal rights, the restriction or widening of the law on abortion, justice for refugees, the control of the police, or transport policy. Those powerfully determined to press their particular concerns on such an issue may well vote for candidates who agree with them, irrespective of party; they will make more impact under a system such as STV than they possibly can under one with only single-member constituencies. The opportunities provided by STV and any other system favourable to minorities must have a salutary effect on the force a central party office can exert upon local candidates; the central office has both less incentive and less power to compel them to toe the party line on every issue.

Thus, in respect of the first component of our twofold criterion for who should represent a multi-member constituency, that minorities, when sufficiently large, should gain representation, STV fully satisfies it: it guarantees representation for minorities to the greatest degree to which any possible electoral system is capable of doing.

CHAPTER 12

How to do Better than STV

A DVOCATES of STV usually appeal to the useless concept of the wasted vote; all that is wasted by such appeals is time. The definition of a wasted vote that is tacitly invoked is that a vote is wasted unless it goes towards bringing about the election of one of the candidates; a vote that, under STV, is transferred to a candidate who eventually secures election is therefore not wasted, on this definition. When the definition is applied to votes under the plurality system, it will follow that everyone who failed to vote for the winning candidate wasted his vote, even if he had no chance, by voting otherwise *under that system*, of bringing about a result he would have liked better.

On this definition, however, there is no reason to say that a wasted vote is a bad thing. Of course, if a voter knew *for certain* what the outcome of the election would be, whether he voted or not, he would not trouble to go to the polling station; since he does not, he has good reason to do whatever he thinks most likely to have a chance of producing a result that will please him. Proponents of STV argue that, even if, under it, a voter does not contribute to bringing about the outcome he principally desires, he will be consoled by the thought that his vote has contributed to the election of one of the candidates. But a voter whose ballot-paper was redistributed to the candidate whom he ranked fifth, and who thereupon attained the quota, will feel very little consolation if he realizes that, under a more equitable system, the candidate whom he ranked highest would have been elected. A voter who placed highest in his order of preference a candidate who remained live until the final stage of the assessment process, only to be defeated at that stage, will have nothing to console him at all: his high ranking of the candidates whom he placed second and third, and who, though highly deserving of election, may have been eliminated at early stages, will never have been taken into account. The concept of the wasted vote has motivated the mechanism of redistributing votes from eliminated candidates and from those who attain the quota; it is naive to attach any importance to it as defining an advantage of STV.

The ability of STV, greatly superior to that of other systems that have been used, to secure representation for minorities, is, on the other hand, a genuine and a salient advantage. It means that STV successfully accomplishes the first component of our dual criterion for the election of true representatives of a multi-member constituency; for this reason, it must be rated superior to any system that does not satisfy that part of the criterion. It is by means of its mechanism of redistributing votes that STV secures representation for minorities; it does not follow that no other mechanism can have the same effect.

How is STV to be judged in the light of the second component of our criterion—that, given that minorities are to be represented by elected candidates, the remaining seats (if any) should go to the most generally popular candidates? When the voting is strongly clumped, the result of an election under STV is likely to be to a great extent fair: those candidates will be elected who ought to be elected under a just system. The same applies when there are individual candidates who attract a very large measure of support, in the sense of being ranked highest by a number of voters exceeding or falling only just below the quota. This will not always happen, however; and then STV is often highly unsatisfactory. A real example, in which STV was far from being at its worst, is provided by an election that took place in West Belfast in April 1925. Four candidates were to be elected, and 49,484 votes were cast, yielding a quota of 9,897. There were seven candidates: these, with their parties and the numbers of voters ranking them highest, were:

Devlin	Nationalist	17,558
Woods	Independent Unionist	11,071
Lynn	Unionist	8,371
Burn	Labour Unionist	4,808
McConville	Republican	3,146
Dickson	Unionist	3,133
McMullan	Labour	2,869

There was little clumping; STV was used, and the winning candidates were Devlin, Woods, Lynn, and McMullan. The assessment process went through six stages. We do not, of course, know just how the voters ranked the candidates on their ballot-papers; a plausible reconstruction would rank the candidates in the following order, according to their Borda scores:

Burn
Devlin
Woods
Dickson
McMullan
McConville
Lynn

Lynn was also, on this reconstruction, the Condorcet tail, every other candidate being preferred by a majority to him. If the reconstruction is roughly correct, therefore, Lynn was extremely lucky to be elected, and did not deserve to be. If Borda scores are accepted as an index of a candidate's general acceptability, Burn should have been elected in place of Lynn, and would have been under a straight Borda system. STV takes account, selectively, of second and third preferences, but of fourth or fifth preferences only when the assessment process needs to go through very many stages;* the high degree of Lynn's unpopularity with many of the voters was therefore masked. Burn suffered, by contrast, from the fact that the large number of Lynn's supporters who (according to the reconstruction) ranked him second was represented by a small total value of votes when Lynn's surplus was redistributed after his attainment of the quota at the fourth stage. This, though very far from an extreme example, well illustrates the erratic operation of STV, which rests on no clear principle and cannot be relied on to bring about the election of the most generally acceptable candidates.

* Sometimes a great number of stages is needed. Thus, in the election under STV held in February 1987 in the Dublin South-East constituency, the four members returned to the Dáil (Irish Parliament) obtained the quota at the first, twelfth, fourteenth, and fifteenth stages.

Absurd claims are made for STV by its advocates. Enid Lakeman, a well-known propagandist on its behalf, was still asserting in her book *Power to Elect* of 1982 that it allowed for no advantage to be gained by tactical voting, although the inability of any electoral system to do this had been proved in 1973. Under any reasonable electoral system, we expect a small change in the way the votes are cast to make a difference only in a certain direction, if it makes any difference at all. The voter may not know whether his decision to vote in one way rather than another will make any difference at all; but he ought to know, with a high degree of probability, *what* difference it will make if it makes any. Under STV, he cannot know this; his intuitions in the matter give him little guidance.

The assessment process of STV cannot be called chaotic in the strict sense, because its 'initial conditions'—the ballot-papers submitted by the voters—allow of a precise description and yield a determinate outcome. It may, however, be said to be quasi-chaotic, in that small changes at the initial stage may be magnified into huge changes at later stages, because they cause different candidates to be eliminated, and that in turn may result in a big variation in the allocation of votes at subsequent stages, owing to the differing redistributions of votes from one candidate and from another. The result of entering any particular ranking on one's ballot-paper therefore becomes unpredictable: a voter is hard put to it to know whether or not he is doing any good for himself by voting sincerely or in any other way.

To grasp the extent to which this is true, we may study the possible effects of a change of vote by just over one-tenth of a percent of the voters. Assume that four seats are to be filled, and there are 99,995 voters, yielding a quota of 20,000. There are eight candidates, A to H. Just 100 voters intend to rank A highest, followed by D; they then change their minds, and reverse the order of these two candidates, leaving their rankings otherwise the same, which we may suppose originally to have been A D B C G F E H. What could they expect the effect of such a change upon the eventual outcome to be under a reasonable electoral system?

Their change of mind affects only A and D. It might therefore seem plausible to suggest that, if their altered votes had any effect at all, it could only be to bring about the election of D in place of A. This, however, would be to assume that no candidate can be affected favourably or adversely, as regards the outcome, by a change in voters' rankings that does not affect that candidate, and this is too strong an assumption. It seems reasonable at least to say that, if the change in the 100 voters' rankings makes any difference at all, it ought either to make one favourable to D, or one unfavourable to A, or one both favourable to D and unfavourable to A; and that in the last case no other candidate ought to be affected, and in any case not more than one other. If a voter, contemplating such a change as that we are imagining to be made by our 100 voters, cannot feel assured that its effect will be of one of these kinds, how can he be even reasonably confident that he is wise to make it?

Let us suppose, first, that, if the 100 voters were *not* to make the change, the stages in the STV assessment process would go as in the table below. A figure is italicized if it exceeds the quota, indicating the election of the candidate concerned. A figure is bracketed if, at that stage, the candidate in question is eliminated. A dash indicates that the candidate has either attained the quota or been eliminated.

A	B	C	D	E	F	G	H
20,004	19,000	12,046	9,595	9,850	10,050	9,670	9,780
——	19,000	12,046	(9,599)	9,850	10,050	9,670	9,780
——	23,700	16,945	——	9,850	10,050	9,670	9,780
——	——	20,645	——	9,850	10,050	9,670	9,780
——	——	——	——	9,850	10,050	10,315	(9,780)
——	——	——	——	(10,050)	14,850	15,095	——
——	——	——	——	——	19,300	20,695	——

Thus A, B, C, and G would be elected.

Now suppose that the 100 voters *do* change their minds, as indicated. The assessment process may then proceed as follows:

A	B	C	D	E	F	G	H
19,904	19,000	12,046	9,695	9,850	10,050	(9,670)	9,780
19,904	19,000	(12,046)	12,095	12,250	12,349	——	12,351
19,904	19,000	——	20,095	15,250	12,349	——	13,397
19,934	19,020	——	——	15,275	(12,359)	——	13,407
19,993	19,320	——	——	22,275	——	——	18,407
19,993	19,520	——	——	——	——	——	20,482
20,393	19,602	——	——	——	——	——	——

This time, the successful candidates are A, D, E, and H. The elevation of D above A in the lists of 100 voters has not harmed A as regards the eventual outcome, but has benefited D by causing him to be elected where he would not have been before; but it appears impossible to say whether D is replacing B, C, or G. Not one, but three candidates, none of whom is **A**, have lost their seats as a result of the change: **E** and **H** have benefited to the extent of being elected, while **B**, **C**, and **G** have all suffered by failing to gain the seats they would otherwise have won; and yet **B**, **C**, **E**, **G**, and **H** were none of them affected by the change of preferences. The change has not affected the outcome in any of the three ways that appeared reasonable on first principles, in that, while it has benefited **D** without harming **A**, it has affected, not one, but five other candidates. It is easy to understand the mechanics of the effect. The postponement of **A**'s eventual success has meant the elimination of **G** at stage 1, so that, instead of a very small number of **C**'s votes being redistributed to **G**, all 12,046 of them are divided among **D**, **E**, and **H**, conferring success upon these candidates at once or later. In the previous case, shown in the earlier table, **D** was eliminated, and 4,700 of his votes went to **B**; this time, since **D** has attained the quota, **B** receives only 20 of his votes. This illustrates how the sequential redistribution of votes under STV can magnify the effect of a slight change in the initial allocation of the votes. To understand the mechanism of this is not to recognize its effects as just: if the outcome was fair in the first instance, that which occurred when the 100 voters changed their minds cannot have been, and conversely.

The effect of the change of mind on the part of the 100 voters about the relative merits of **A** and **D** may be quite different from that shown in the second table. Let us suppose that, without the change of mind, the assessment process would go as in the first table; it may nevertheless be that, as a result of the change of mind, it would go as follows:

A	B	C	D	E	F	G	H
19,904	19,000	12,046	9,695	9,850	10,050	(9,670)	9,780
19,904	19,000	(12,046)	12,095	12,250	12,349	——	12,351
19,904	19,000	——	12,095	15,250	*20,349*	——	13,397
19,904	19,000	——	(12,095)	15,599	——	——	13,397
19,904	*24,922*	——	——	*21,772*	——	——	13,397
21,598	——	——	——	——	——	——	18,397

Here the change of mind by 100 voters in favour of **D** and to the disadvantage of **A** has again had a dramatic effect: but it has left the positions of **A** and **D**, in respect of the final outcome, unaltered. **A** is still elected; **D** still fails to gain election. Instead, **C**, **E**, **F**, and **G** are affected: **C** and **G** lose their seats, and **E** and **F** gain seats that they did not win before; the overall result is that **A**, **B**, **E**, and **F** are elected, in place of **A**, **B**, **C**, and **G**. This time the elimination of **C** has worked to the advantage of **F** rather than of **D**, owing to the fact that, in this case, **F** rather than **D** is the second choice of two-thirds of **C**'s supporters. **D**'s supporters now receive far less compensation for his elimination than before the change of mind, since **C** has already been eliminated. The effect, in this case, of a revision of their rankings in favour of **D** as against **A** by a mere 100 voters could not be expected from a reasonable electoral system; it would certainly dismay those voters if they realized what the effect of their change of mind had been.

An example in which the reversal of the positions of **A** and **D** by 100 voters will have the effect they least desire is as follows. If they do not reverse the positions of those two candidates, but list **A** highest, the assessment process may go through the following stages:

A	B	C	D	E	F	G	H
15,004	19,000	13,296	(9,595)	11,100	11,300	9,670	11,030
24,599	19,000	13,396	——	11,100	11,300	9,670	11,030
——	19,000	13,796	——	11,199	11,300	(9,670)	11,030
——	20,670	15,796	——	13,199	13,300	——	13,030
——	——	15,796	——	13,199	13,670	——	(13,330)
——	——	21,126	——	19,199	15,670	——	——
——	——	——	——	19,323	16,670	——	——

A, B, C, and E are elected. At the final stage, E does not
obtain the quota, but is declared elected because he has at
that stage more votes than the sole other hopeful candidate
F.

When the 100 voters reverse the positions of A and D,
however, the assessment may go as follows:

A	B	C	D	E	F	G	H
14,904	19,000	13,296	9,695	11,100	11,300	(9,670)	11,030
14,904	20,670	14,046	15,001	11,646	12,152	——	11,676
14,904	——	14,046	15,001	(11,646)	12,726	——	11,672
14,904	——	20,046	15,001	——	15,026	——	15,018
(14,910)	——	——	15,001	——	15,046	——	15,038
——	——	——	19,861	——	20,076	——	20,058

This time B, C, F, and H have been elected instead of A,
B, C, and E. The result of the change in the lists of the 100
voters has been to prevent the election of A, without doing
any ultimate good to D. Under a more reasonable system
than STV, only A would lose his seat, to be replaced by
some one other candidate, whereas, in this case, E has also
suffered, the two being replaced by F and H.

The perversity that STV is capable of displaying may be

driven home by one more example. Suppose that, before the change of mind, the assessment process had gone as follows:

A	B	C	D	E	F	G	H
10,433	*21,001*	13,936	9,595	11,639	12,051	9,670	11,670
10,933	——	14,437	(9,595)	11,639	12,051	9,670	11,670
(10,933)	——	16,032	——	11,639	12,051	17,670	11,670
——	——	*20,643*	——	11,639	12,051	*21,270*	14,392
——	——	——	——	(11,639)	12,051	——	16,305
——	——	——	——	——	19,690	——	*20,305*

The effect of the change of mind by the 100 voters might then be as follows:

A	B	C	D	E	F	G	H
10,333	*21,001*	13,936	9,695	11,639	12,051	9,670	11,670
10,833	——	14,437	9,695	11,639	12,051	(9,670)	11,670
20,503	——	14,437	9,695	11,639	12,051	——	11,670
——	——	14,650	(9,859)	11,639	12,051	——	11,796
——	——	16,300	——	19,848	12,051	——	(11,796)
——	——	17,596	——	*21,848*	*20,551*	——	——

The effect of the change of mind has been that, where **B**, **C**, **G**, and **H** would have been elected, **A**, **B**, **E**, and **F** are. The promotion of **D** above **A** on the ballot-papers of 100 voters has not benefited **D**, who still fails to be elected; but it has benefited **A**, who now wins a seat which he would not have won when he was better thought of by those voters. This is an example of STV's possession of the feature we have already noted as attaching to AV, non-monotonicity: ranking a candidate highest may diminish his chances. Furthermore, the election of **A** has not displaced just one third candidate, but has deprived three, **C**, **G**, and **H**, of their seats, while **E** and **F**, who, like **C**, **G**, and **H**, retain exactly the same position in the voters' order of preferences, gain seats they would not have obtained before. The 100 voters who changed their minds are certainly better off than before, for now their second choice, **A**, has been elected, whereas previously neither **D** nor **A** was. But the change is one they could not have expected, and the method of obtaining it bizarre.

The relentless, and often grossly misleading propaganda on behalf of STV makes it hard for the assertion that STV is a quasi-chaotic system to appear credible unless backed by examples. The reaction to such examples on the part of proponents of STV is predictable, namely that they will be very rare. As Charles Dodgson (Lewis Carroll) remarked:

I am quite prepared to be told with regard to the cases I have here proposed, as I have already been told with regard to others, 'Oh, *that* is an extreme case: it could never really happen!' Now I have observed that this answer is always given instantly, with perfect confidence, and without any examination of the details of the proposed case. It must therefore rest on some general principle: the mental process being probably something like this—'I have formed a theory. This case contradicts my theory. *Therefore* this is an extreme case, and would never occur in practice.'

The Royal Commission on Electoral Reform of 1910 already observed that the order in which candidates are eliminated under STV can make a large difference to the outcome; this is the source of its erratic operation. The gap between the total of votes assigned to a candidate at the stage when he is eliminated and the next higher total assigned at that stage to another candidate may be very small; this is why the votes of a small number of electors may have so great an effect upon the eventual outcome. In the examples given above, the gap was taken to be less than 100, which is why a change of mind by 100 voters could have a devastating effect. It may happen seldom that a crucial gap is as small as this; it will happen quite often that it is only a few hundred votes. It is not in the least bizarre to suppose that the elimination of one candidate should have a decisively different effect upon the resulting redistribution of votes from that of a different candidate, and hence upon the consequent course of the assessment process.

STV is quasi-chaotic because it takes into account only the first choices of some voters, and the second, third, or even fourth choices of others, giving them as much weight as the first choices. It takes account of only the first choices of those voters who support candidates who survive until the final stage, whether successful or unsuccessful; and for this reason, strong support for a candidate, manifested by his being the second choice of many voters, may simply be disregarded, while similar support for another is given full weight. Such support will also be disregarded when the candidate is the first choice of only a small number of voters, and hence is soon eliminated, while one who just escapes elimination may later pick up votes in large numbers by redistribution.

It would be easy to devise preference scales for the voters that accorded with the results of the assessment process in our four examples before and after the change of mind by the 100 voters; but the labour is unnecessary in order to demonstrate that STV must often produce results widely at variance with the Borda scores. A reversal on the part of 100 voters in their ranking of A and D could result in a change in the Borda scores of only those two candidates; 100 points more for D and 100 points less for A. It therefore could not have the same effect upon which four candidates obtained the highest Borda scores as it did upon the outcome of the election under STV in the examples. STV is a thoroughly fallacious guide to which candidates are the most generally acceptable. Its claim to constitute the best electoral system should be unhesitatingly rejected.

It is not here being argued that STV has any inherent *bias* towards candidates of a particular type or political persuasion, only that it is exceptionally erratic in its operation, producing results that are virtually random.

How, then, can a better system be found for elections to multi-member constituencies? We should not hunt around among systems used in practice or even those proposed, but recall that our model is DIY: we must *devise* a better system. Our criterion for who ought to be elected was a dual one; we must therefore create a system in which one criterion is superimposed upon another. (The composite system suggested for elections to single-member constituencies was one relying on two criteria.) We wish to use Borda scores to determine the most generally popular candidates. Hence, as under STV, voters must be instructed to rank candidates in order of preference on their ballot-papers. They should probably be urged to rank all of them, but permitted, if they wish, to omit some candidates from their ranking. From the ballot-papers, Borda scores will be calculated for all the candidates; candidates omitted from a voter's ranking will be treated as if he had bracketed them equal below all the candidates he has ranked. (If a voter ranks all the candidates, he will contribute 0, 1, and 2 points respectively to the Borda scores of the three candidates he ranks lowest. Hence one who leaves three candidates out of his ranking will be taken as having contributed 1 point—the average—to the scores of each of them.)

The criterion of Borda scores is, however, to be overridden by that of solid support by a minority. When five seats are to be filled, a minority of voters will be deemed to be entitled to the election of one candidate if it is greater than a sixth of the total number of votes cast, and to the election of two candidates if it is greater than a third of that number. STV protects not only minorities, but majorities too. A set of voters amounting to three times the quota—and thus, in a five-member constituency, to a bare majority—will, if it gives solid support to a set of three or more candidates, be sure under STV of getting three candidates elected. Our purpose, however, is to secure representation for sufficiently large minorities, not to give what may be disproportionate representation to majorities; we therefore need not imitate this feature of STV. In a four-member constituency, we should take account of minorities amounting to more than one-fifth or more than two-fifths of the total number of those voting; in a three-member constituency, only to those amounting to more than a quarter of those voting.

Let us suppose that the constituency is to return five Members to Parliament. Having calculated the Borda scores of the candidates, the tellers' first task must be to discover whether solid support has been given by any sufficiently large minority of voters to some set of candidates. This they should do directly, not by the mechanism of redistributing votes from successful or eliminated candidates. They have first to determine whether any single candidates have been ranked highest by more than a sixth of the voters: if so, they will register them as having been elected. If, at any stage of the assessment process, all five seats have been filled, the process will of course be brought to an end and the result announced. Next, the tellers will have to determine whether any pair of candidates, one of whom has already been registered as elected, has solid support from more than a third of the voters: if so, the other member of the pair must be registered as elected. Now the tellers must scrutinize all pairs of candidates neither of whom has been registered as elected, to see if any such pair has solid support from more than a sixth of the voters. If so, that one of the pair must be registered as elected who has the higher Borda score of the two.

Unless all five seats have now been filled, the tellers must now consider sets of three candidates, one of whom has already been registered as elected. If any such set receives solid support from more than a third of the voters, that one of the other two members who has the higher Borda score will be registered as elected. The tellers will then consider sets of three, none of whom has yet been registered as elected. If any such set is solidly supported by more than a sixth of the voters, that one who has the highest Borda score must be registered as elected, or, if the support comes from more than a third of the voters, those two members of the set who have the highest Borda scores must be so registered. If the five seats have not yet been filled, the tellers must proceed in the same way to consider sets of four and of five candidates having solid support from more than a sixth of those voting. There are five seats to be filled. Some political parties may have put up as many as five candidates, perhaps hoping to get them all elected; it may therefore be necessary to consider sets of five candidates. No party is likely to put up more candidates than can be elected; since minorities not defined by adherence to a political party are very unlikely to be solidly committed to more candidates than there are seats to be filled, there will be no need to consider sets of six or more candidates.

If the process of scrutinizing sets of candidates given solid support by groups of voters amounting to more than a sixth of the total number of votes cast does not succeed in identifying candidates to fill all the five seats, the remaining seats will then be filled by those candidates, among those not yet registered as elected, who have the highest Borda scores. The final results will then be announced. This system may be labelled QBS (for 'Quota/Borda system'). It may seem highly laborious for the tellers (computers would greatly lighten their task, as usual). It would indeed be laborious for them, but considerably less so than STV, to which few object for this reason. In practice, most sets of two to five candidates could be very quickly dismissed from consideration; there cannot be more than five minorities comprising more than a sixth of the voters. The system would need to be explained very carefully to the electors, since it is based on an idea unfamiliar to them, that of a group of voters giving solid support to a set of candidates. The idea, once explained, is not difficult to grasp, however, and the justice of relying on it would readily become apparent.

Various details of the system are capable of variation. Under STV, a sufficiently large group of voters giving solid support to a set of candidates will, in general, succeed in getting elected that one of them who is most popular with the group: under QBS, as described, the candidate in that set who will be elected will be the one most popular with the electorate in general. This appears to me to be equitable; but the contrary opinion may well be held. If desired, it would be possible to compute restricted Borda scores, on the basis solely of those ballot-papers submitted by members of the minority giving solid support to the set of candidates; only those candidates belonging to the set would need to be taken into account. The candidate registered as elected would then be the one with the highest restricted Borda score. Another problem arises when sets of candidates given solid support overlap. Suppose that one group of voters, amounting to more than a sixth but less than a third of the electorate, gives solid support to the pair consisting of **A** and **B**, while another group, also forming more than a sixth but less than a third of the electorate, gives solid support to the trio comprising **A**, **C**, and **D**. According to the foregoing stipulations, if **A** has a higher Borda score than **B**, he will be elected, and the minority giving solid support to the trio will have no claim to have any further representative; but, if **B** has the higher Borda score, both he and a member of the trio (who might be **A**) will be elected. In order to economize on representatives of minorities, it would be possible to introduce a rule that, in such a case, **A** should be elected as representing both minorities, irrespective of Borda scores. If QBS were to find favour with people anxious for electoral reform, these and other details could be negotiated.

QBS will not produce the same erratic results as STV, because its operation is quite different. It lacks, however, the property which advocates of STV insist on as its great merit. Under STV, supporters of a candidate **A** will not always be doing their best for him by ranking him first on their ballot-papers; but, having ranked him first, they cannot affect his chances by their choice of the candidate they rank second or third. This is not true of QBS. Suppose that there are five seats to be filled, and that a small number of voters, who have ranked **A** first and **B** second, are uncertain whether to rank **C** or **D** third. It may be that if they choose **C** to rank third, the trio **A**, **B**, and **C** will have the solid support of a little more than a sixth of those voting; **A** will then be elected, as having the highest Borda score of the three. If those voters rank **D** third, however, they may reduce the solid support for **A**, **B**, and **C** to just under a sixth of those voting; and in this case none of the trio may eventually be elected. By their choice of the candidate they rank third, those few voters have deprived their favourite candidate **A** of his chance to be elected.

This feature of QBS forms the chief incentive it supplies for tactical voting. Suppose that certain voters are agreed in wanting either **A** or **B** to be elected, and in disapproving of **C**; but they know that a sizable group of electors is likely to give solid support to the trio **A**, **B**, and **C**. Having all ranked either **A** or **B** first on their ballot-papers, and the other of the two second, the voters who disapprove of **C** may yet, for strategic reasons, decide to rank **C** third. Their hope is that, by doing so, they will raise the number of voters giving solid support to **A**, **B**, and **C** to the required proportion of those voting, and hence secure the election of either **A** or **B**. They are taking the risk of bringing about the election of **C**; they will presumably have estimated whether it was worth while by guessing whether **A** or **B** was likely to be more popular than **C** with the electorate as a whole. The effect of strategic voting of this kind will not usually greatly distort the equity of the result.

We have, in QBS, a system at least as readily workable as STV, retaining its great advantage but free of the inequitable results of its haphazard operation. We have also a system that realizes, as far as is possible, the twin objectives we laid down for elections to multi-member constituencies. It is up to the reader to decide whether or not he wishes to challenge those objectives, and, if not, whether he can devise any better means of attaining them.

CHAPTER 13

Proportional
Representation

I N this book, we have concentrated primarily on how to achieve true representation for local electorates and for the national electorate as a whole, and secondarily on how to discourage tactical voting. A choice of an electoral system should be made with an eye to other questions as well. To ask whether any one system chooses the most representative candidates is to treat the candidates as given; but which candidates stand for election depends upon the number and identity of the political parties that sponsor them. We must therefore also ask which effects various electoral systems have upon the parties. Do they encourage parties to adopt platforms that approximate to the political centre, or ones that appeal to holders of more extreme opinions? Do they create strong incentives for parties to maintain their cohesion, or do they tempt them to break into fragments? Do they make it hard to launch a new party, or vain to keep a small one in existence, or do they, conversely, foster a proliferation of parties whose policies often differ only marginally from those of some of their rivals?

The answers to these questions are connected with one

another. It is well known that the plurality system, used subject to the constituency principle, has the effect of creating a strong incentive to the political parties to remain united, however torn by internal dissension they may be. This is another defect of that system. The ideal for an electoral system is to offer no incentive either for cohesion or for fragmentation: it is best if parties cohere only to the extent that, and for so long as, their members can co-operate with one another without animosity or accusations of disloyalty. For the same reason that it places a premium on party unity, the plurality system without a dual vote severely disadvantages small or new parties: in Britain, only the Labour Party ever succeeded in overcoming that disadvantage, and then only owing to the help it received from the Liberals. Any form of proportional representation, or any system whose effect at the national level is to approximate proportionality, will discourage small parties much less, if at all; sometimes, indeed, strict proportional representation results in a plethora of political parties, thereby creating a strong motive for imposing a threshold.

A system that ensures that there will be only a few parties thereby generates an impetus that drives most of them towards the centre. A large left-wing party, having no serious rival to its left, feels confident that it can safely move its platform to the right, nearer to the centre, relying on there being no other place for those of its supporters who disapprove of the shift to go. The same holds good, with 'left' and 'right' interchanged, of a large right-wing party. This does not mean that policies will stay constant, since the centre is not a fixed point. Most people falsely believe that their political opinions—and their opinions on many other matters—remain invariant over long periods of time: what actually remain invariant are their positions along the left/right or the progressive/conservative axis, which go to form their images of their own personalities. But, while their views continue to occupy the same positions on the axis, their substance may shift a great deal, because what is perceived as being the centre swings in one direction or the other, taking with it all other positions on the axis defined by their relations to the centre. This explains why a newspaper editorial will often state that 'nobody' believes something which that newspaper was itself propounding only two or three years earlier. The centre is never *identified* with the prevailing policies or with the ideology of the existing régime; but its absolute position is powerfully affected by them, since it is never perceived as being at a great distance from them. The views of those currently in power are hardly ever considered as extreme: so if a government adopts policies that would formerly have been regarded as extreme, the centre shifts in that direction, so that those policies are no longer seen as being extreme.

A system that severely limits the number of parties capable of competing electorally, and provides a strong incentive for the few that can to shift their policies towards the centre, robs many electors of the chance to vote for candidates who truly represent their views. Under any system of PR, small parties have a chance of getting a few candidates elected; and since there will therefore less often be parties that lack any rivals the other side of them from the centre, they will not be able to count on disgruntled electors having no place to go. STV by no means always secures for small parties the representation they would obtain under PR as normally applied. Thus in the Irish general election of 1989 the Progressive Democrats obtained 5.5 per cent of first choices on the ballot-papers, but won only 6 seats out of 166 in the Dáil (3.6 per cent). Nevertheless, STV offers a far better chance for small parties than does the plurality system in single-member constituencies.

In constituency elections, systems based on Condorcet's, Copeland's, or Borda's criterion will be far more favourable to candidates occupying moderate positions than will the plurality system or AV, and will likewise be unfavourable to those representing extreme positions on the left/right axis. This will itself create an impetus towards the centre, though not as strong as the plurality system; electors whose views lie far from the centre will not in the same way be deprived of the chance of expressing them. When each constituency returns only a single member, the probability is that the most representative candidate will be one with moderate views, and the bias towards moderation can be corrected only by adopting either the dual-vote device or multi-member constituencies. When candidates can realistically be arranged along a left/right axis, Condorcet's criterion is in fact the more favourable to moderates than Borda's, and creates a stronger impetus towards the centre. When the electors are arranged along the axis, a party's aim in a single-member constituency will be to capture the vote of the median elector. Admittedly, the use of Borda's criterion can result in the defeat of a highly contentious candidate even if he commands an absolute majority of first choices, provided that there is another candidate who has very general approval. The criterion treats moderate and contentious candidates even-handedly. What it favours is widespread popularity, which is not the same thing as the support of the median elector, as may be illustrated by the following simple example:

2,000	3,000	1,000	3,000	2,000
A	B	C	D	E
B	A	B	C	D
C	C	D	B	C
D	D	A	E	B
E	E	E	A	A

C is the Condorcet leader, and is the first choice of the median voter; but B has the higher Borda count, with 29,000 points to C's 27,000.

Some of those who advocate electoral reform favour the dual-vote device; most of them, however, believe that the constituency principle should be retained. A curious anomaly, never remarked upon, can be discerned in the views of this majority of electoral reformers. They are contemptuous of the idea that, in constituency elections, the ballot-papers should allow the voters to express only their first choices among the candidates: they favour systems such as AV or STV which allow voters to express their preferences between other candidates, and which, in determining the winner or winners of the election, take such lower preferences into account. These electoral reformers are one and all in favour of proportional representation at the national level. Yet, when it comes to representation of the political parties in Parliament, they do not think that account should be taken of anything but the first choices of the electors among the parties. Seats in Parliament should be allotted to a political party in accordance with the proportion of electors who rate that party as the best: it is irrelevant what preferences they may have among the other parties.

This is surely an anomaly. If it is wrong to take account only of voters' first choices between the candidates in a constituency election, why is it not equally wrong to take account only of electors' first choices between the parties when determining how seats are to be allotted to the parties in Parliament? There can surely be no rational answer to this question, and yet the question is never raised.

The reason for the anomaly is simple. Advocates of electoral reform are not in the least concerned with securing the right representatives for the constituencies. They know, of course, that who is elected to represent a constituency will depend on the electoral system in use: if they thought that the same people would be elected whatever system were in force, they would not trouble to urge a change in that system. But they do not think it matters. Their sole concern is to achieve proportional representation, or some approximation to it. Provided that parliamentary seats are distributed between the political parties as they believe they ought to be distributed, it is a matter of indifference to them whether those elected to represent the various constituencies are truly representative of those constituencies or not. They do not argue for the replacement of the plurality system by some other because they are concerned to obtain for the constituencies MPs who will more faithfully represent the views and interests of the local electorate than those elected under the plurality system. They argue for replacing it solely because, given the constituency principle, it will result in a distribution of parliamentary seats approximating more closely to the proportional distribution for which they long than the plurality system does or can ever do.

Voters in a general election, casting their votes to determine who shall be elected to represent their constituency, of course care strongly about the resulting composition of Parliament, when, as in Britain, that will decide who shall form the government, and hence the policies that will be put into effect for the next four or five years. But they do not care *only* about that: if they did, the simplest method would be to turn the whole country into a single constituency, as in Israel. Local voters care very much who is elected to represent them; and they are right to do so. It is for this reason that, when thinking about electoral reform, we should give much attention to the method of selecting constituency representatives, and to who, given the preferences of the voters, ought to be selected; it is for this reason that the greater part of this book has been devoted to these questions.

We saw, when studying them, that, to determine the most representative candidate, account has to be taken, not only of which candidate is each voter's first choice, but also of voters' preferences between candidates neither of whom they prefer to all others. There is no reason whatever why the same should not hold good of electors' preferences between the political parties when, at the national level, we are concerned to judge how a truly representative Parliament should be divided between the parties. Suppose that, in some country, there are four national parties: the Socialist Party, the Moderate Party, the Conservative Party, and the Ultra Party. And suppose that, when electors are asked to nominate that party which each prefers to all others, 45 per cent nominate the Socialists, 10 per cent the

Moderates, 35 per cent the Conservatives, and 10 per cent the Ultras. Then scarcely any advocate of PR would doubt that Parliamentary seats should be distributed among the parties in the same proportions. Thus, if there are 600 seats in Parliament, these should go to the various parties in the following numbers:

Socialists	—	270
Moderates	—	60
Conservatives	—	210
Ultras	—	60

Since the Moderate Party has the same level of (first-choice) support in the country as does the Ultra Party, each gains the same number of seats in Parliament.

However, if, instead, the electors were given the opportunity to rank all four parties in order of preference, a very different picture might well emerge. We may, to avoid complications, suppose that all Socialist supporters prefer the Moderates to the Conservatives and the Conservatives to the Ultras; conversely, we may suppose that all Ultra supporters prefer the Conservatives to the Moderates and the Moderates to the Socialists. Assume, further, that all supporters of the Moderate Party regard the Ultra Party as the worst, and that two in five of them think the Socialists preferable to the Conservatives, and the other three in five conversely. Finally, let us assume that all Conservative supporters prefer the Moderates to the Socialists, while two in seven of them think that even the Ultras are better than the Socialists, the rest rating the Ultras the worst. The electorate is thus divided into six groups, according to their preference scales between the parties, as follows (the figures at the head of each column indicate the percentage of the electorate formed by each group):

45%	4%	6%	10%	25%	10%
S	M	M	C	C	U
M	S	C	M	M	C
C	C	S	U	S	M
U	U	U	S	U	S

If these rankings are sincere, then, among the parties, the Moderate Party is the Condorcet leader, being preferred to the Conservative Party by 55 per cent of the electorate, to the Socialist Party by a different 55 per cent, and to the Ultra Party by an overwhelming 90 per cent. The Ultra Party, conversely, is the Condorcet tail, since 90 per cent prefer the Conservative Party to it, the same 90 per cent prefer the Moderate Party, and 80 per cent prefer the Socialists. In the light of these preferences, the allocation of the same number of Parliamentary seats to the Moderate and Ultra Parties is flagrantly inequitable and unrepresentative of opinion in the country. Yet it is what virtually all advocates of proportional representation would unreflectively assert to be right.

Let us compute the Borda scores per 100 voters of the four parties. They come to:

Socialists	— 174
Moderates	— 200
Conservatives	— 186
Ultras	— 40

The Moderates emerge as the most generally popular party, despite their low level of first-choice support; the Ultra Party, unsurprisingly, is the least popular. The Conservative

Party comes out as marginally more popular than the Socialist Party; it is, after all, preferred to it by a slender majority of 51 per cent among the electorate as a whole. If seats in Parliament were allotted in proportion to Borda scores, the figures just given would indicate the number of seats each party would obtain, since 100 voters will between them distribute 600 Borda points. It would, however, require an extremely sophisticated electorate to accept as equitable such a distribution of seats, giving more to the Moderate Party than to either the Conservatives or the Socialists. And, indeed, it is doubtful whether it would be equitable. We have, in this chapter, challenged the standard assumption of proponents of PR, that seats in Parliament should be distributed among the political parties *in proportion to* the level of their first-choice support. It is much more tendentious to call in question the weaker assumption, that the greatest number (not, in general, the absolute majority) of seats should go to the party with the highest first-choice support.

A compromise can be attained by using *weighted* Borda scores, comprising a substantial bonus for being an elector's first choice. In the present instance, with four political parties, this could be achieved by awarding 1 point to a party for being third in an elector's ranking, 2 points for being second, and 6 points for standing highest in his ranking. This would yield the following weighted scores per 100 voters:

Socialists	— 309
Moderates	— 230
Conservatives	— 291
Ultras	— 70

If seats were distributed in proportion to these weighted scores, each party would obtain:

Socialists	—	206 seats
Moderates	—	153 seats
Conservatives	—	194 seats
Ultras	—	47 seats

The Ultras have suffered from their general unpopularity, the Moderates have gained immensely from their general acceptability, the Conservatives have lost slightly, and the Socialists more heavily, but they have retained their position as the party with the greatest number of seats. To my eye, this outcome is in a high degree equitable.

The appropriate value of the bonus will depend upon the number of political parties between which seats are to be distributed. With four of them, the foregoing suggestion is probably about right; but the reader who has accepted the general argument of this chapter must experiment with various imaginary situations and different hypothetical values of the bonus to discover which he regards as yielding a result that duly accords with the distribution of electors' preferences between the parties.

An allocation of parliamentary seats between the parties in proportion to weighted Borda scores will favour a moderate party which is many voters' second choice, such as that so named in the example. When the electorate is split between mighty opposites, neither of which commands a majority, it surely accords with the spirit of democracy that moderate parties should have a substantial place in the legislature, especially one which is the most generally popular party of all, in the sense of being preferred by a majority to each of the other parties taken separately. Conversely, the use of Borda scores (weighted or not) would have an adverse effect on extreme parties like the Ultras in the example; when account is taken of second and third preferences, moderate and extreme parties identify themselves by the pattern of electors' preference scales. There is then no need for any artificial hurdle, like the clumsy device of the 5 per cent threshold in the German system. This is principally intended as a protection from extremist parties; with points given for being an elector's second or third choice, there is protection enough against a party that most electors will rank lowest.

Although widely believed to be the ideal at which electoral reform should aim, proportional representation based on first choices alone is a defective ideal.

It can be objected, with some reason, that the use of weighted Borda scores to assess the fair representation of the parties in Parliament would encourage parties to split. A division of a party into two could indeed bring a dramatic benefit to the representation of the combined two splinters over that of the previously unified party. Suppose that the Socialist Party divides into the Workers' Party and the Labour Party, and that the preference scales of the electors, by percentages, are then as follows:

20%	25%	4%	6%	10%	25%	10%
W	L	M	M	C	C	U
L	W	L	C	M	M	C
M	M	W	L	U	L	M
C	C	C	W	L	U	L
U	U	U	U	W	W	W

If, for every 100 voters, we compute the Borda scores of the parties, adding a bonus of 3 points per voter for being his first choice, we obtain the following scores:

Workers	— 229
Labour	— 329
Moderates	— 285
Conservatives	— 342
Ultras	— 115

If Parliamentary seats are allotted proportionally to these scores, the result will be:

Workers	— 106 seats
Labour	— 152 seats
Moderates	— 131 seats
Conservatives	— 158 seats
Ultras	— 53 seats

The Workers' and Labour Parties have together obtained 258 seats, 52 more than did the united Socialist Party in the preceding example. Provided that the two fragments contrive to work in harmony with one another, the Socialists have gained a great advantage by dividing themselves into two parties.

Such an advantage is to be gained by small parties as well as large ones. Suppose that the Socialist Party remains united, but that the Moderate Party splits into a Progressive and a Radical Party. The preference scales of the electors are then as follows:

45%	4%	6%	10%	25%	10%
S	R	P	C	C	U
R	P	R	P	P	C
P	S	C	R	R	P
C	C	S	U	S	R
U	U	U	S	U	S

Since there are now five parties, let us raise the bonus for being an elector's first choice from 3 to 5 points; the weighted Borda scores, per 100 electors, will now be:

Socialists	— 444
Radicals	— 269
Progressives	— 281
Conservatives	— 406
Ultras	— 100

and the corresponding parliamentary seats:

Socialists	— 178 seats
Radicals	— 108 seats
Progressives	— 112 seats
Conservatives	— 162 seats
Ultras	— 40 seats

The two fragments into which the Moderate Party has split have between them gained 220 seats, as against the 153 the party would have had if it had remained intact.

If weighted Borda scores were used to determine the just distribution of seats in Parliament, there would have to be an electoral commission charged, among other things, with verifying that any split that occurred in a political party was genuine, and that the fragments had no liaison between each other and were truly separate organizations. If, nevertheless, the system were found to foster purely tactical fragmentation of the parties, it would certainly have to be abandoned. It would be extremely difficult to devise a mechanism to obviate it. One might think of calculating the Borda scores by fictitiously treating all the larger parties as if they were composed of smaller parties of some minimum size: in this way there would be no incentive to them to split in reality, and no disincentive for smaller parties to coalesce. But this idea founders on the difficulty of defining the 'size' of a party. If we define it as the number of electors whose first choice it is, we shall in effect be giving a huge premium to a party's being an elector's first choice: even if we do not weight the Borda scores, the result will be to allot to a large party a much higher proportion of parliamentary seats than its proportion of first choices by the electors. If we treat the Borda score of a party, when it is considered as intact, as constituting its size, we shall be restoring the incentive for fragmentation, which we were seeking to avoid. It does not appear that any electoral mechanism can counter the effect.

It may well be that the fear of such tactically motivated fragmentation is misplaced, however. The formation of two parties out of one is a traumatic event. To give it any colour at all, the two new parties must be to some degree differentiated by their policies; and it will necessarily be hard to avoid some resentment between them. Only one can inherit the organization on the national and the local level: the party funds, the national office, the constituency agents, the local party machine. It may well be, therefore, that parties would be deterred from taking advantage of the increase of seats in Parliament that they could obtain from artificially splitting into two by the concomitant price that they would have to pay for the division; and in this case the use of weighted Borda scores will give a much fairer distribution of parliamentary seats than reliance on electors' first choices alone. This applies, of course, only when fairness is our aim: when, in the spirit of PR, we aim to make Parliament a mirror of national opinion. As we saw in Chapter 3, proponents of the 'Winner Take All' principle pursue an entirely different aim.

CHAPTER 14

The Principles of Electoral Reform

THERE is always a danger in devoting the last chapter of a book to summarizing its whole argument, namely that readers who think their time too valuable to waste on reading the book from cover to cover will content themselves with skimming the final chapter, confident that no author can have anything to tell them that they cannot extract in this economical manner. Such readers usually only half-understand the little that they thus glance at. This chapter cannot serve as a substitute for reading the book; it is meant only as a reminder. Although I have been unable to refrain from expressing personal predilections here and there, I have repeatedly emphasized that my intention has not been to recommend any particular electoral system, but to formulate the principles that ought to govern the way we think about electoral reform: whether it is needed and, if so, how it ought to be carried out. It is then up to the readers to make the resulting decisions. The principles that should guide their thinking, as I see them, can be enumerated as follows:

(1) There are two problems to be solved, not one. That

on which attention is usually concentrated is the composition of Parliament, and especially its lower House (in Britain the House of Commons) by political parties, given the preferences between the parties of the national electorate. The second is equally problematic: by what method we should select representatives of the constituencies. This is not problematic solely in virtue of its effect upon the composition of Parliament: it is problematic *in itself.*

(2) The possibility of adopting the dual-vote device, used in German elections, allows us to think about the two problems separately. The dual-vote device separates the mechanism for selecting representatives of the constituencies from that for determining the composition of Parliament. It thereby violates the constituency principle, that Parliament, or its lower House, should be exclusively composed of constituency representatives. Although it relieves voters of the quandary in which they may be placed by having only a single vote that goes both to select one or more representatives of their own constituencies and to determine the composition of Parliament, its contravention of the constituency principle may be seen as a severe demerit of the dual-vote device: it involves that there will be some MPs not elected to represent any constituency. However distasteful we may find this consequence, we should *not* dismiss the device out of hand at the outset. We should still think about and discuss the two problems separately. We may arrive at a conclusion about the problem of selecting constituency representatives that will by and large satisfy whatever conclusion we reach about the composition of Parliament when the constituency principle is observed. If so, well and good. But the two problems are quite different, and there is no

guarantee that the same electoral mechanism will resolve both. If we fail to find one that does so, we shall have a choice. Either we can find a compromise between a system that will serve one of the two purposes and a system that will serve the other; or we can adopt the dual-vote device to resolve the conflict. At that stage in our thinking, we shall know what the costs of either decision will be; if we reject the dual-vote device before reaching that stage, we shall be choosing blindly.

(3) Each of the two problems should be approached in the same way. We should, in each case, *first* decide what we want, and only after that consider how to get it. Forming a preference for one electoral system over another before first making up our minds what we want an electoral system to do is a recipe for confused thinking on the subject. Deciding what we want an electoral system to do amounts to this. We suppose that we know, in any given instance, what the preferences of the electors are (between the candidates in a constituency, between the parties nationally); we then ask ourselves what, on the basis of those preferences, we think the outcome of the election ought to be. We must frame a precise, not merely a hazy, answer to this question, and one that will cover all cases (all possible distributions of preferences). Only then shall we be in a position to make sensible judgements about the merits of different electoral systems.

(4) The question what we want an electoral system to do is the hard one to answer. If we have formulated a precise answer to it, the second question, what electoral system will achieve what we want, is *usually* comparatively simple.

(5) In answering the second question, we need not confine ourselves to known electoral systems, used in practice

or merely proposed: we can as easily devise one for ourselves.

(6) There are two types of principle for determining the desirable composition of Parliament from the preferences between the political parties of the national electorate: the 'Winner Take All' principle (WTA) and proportional representation (PR). WTA requires that whichever party has the greatest support (is the first choice of the greatest number of electors) should have an absolute majority in Parliament. It has two versions: WW and WP. According to WW, when it has been determined how many seats are to be allotted to the leading party, a disproportionate number of the remaining seats should be given to the party having the second highest level of national support, other parties being accorded only small numbers of seats. According to WP, by contrast, the remaining seats should be distributed among the parties other than that obtaining a majority in Parliament in as close approximation as possible to the proportions of their support in the national electorate. These general ideas, if favoured, would need to be embodied in definite numerical formulas connecting percentages of national electoral support with numbers of parliamentary seats.

(7) Proportional representation, as usually understood, requires that the number of seats in Parliament allotted to each party should, as far as possible, be proportional to the number of electors whose first choice it is. This is frequently modified by a threshold, denying any seats in Parliament to a party that has not attained some fixed minimum percentage of national votes (first choices). A variant, discussed in Chapter 13, is that the number of seats should be proportional to its weighted Borda score, taken over the electorate

as a whole. This should probably give preponderant weight to a party's being an elector's first choice, but will nevertheless give some weight to his preferences between the parties he does not rank highest. Under this variant, a threshold is unlikely to be necessary. Its disadvantage is that it may encourage unnecessary fragmentation of parties.

(8) WTA is recommended on the grounds that it promotes strong and stable government. It certainly does. Under the system obtaining in Britain, where the executive and legislative powers are not separated, it produces a government usually secure in office for the duration of Parliament. It therefore subserves the principle of what has been called 'elective dictatorship': for the lifetime of Parliament, opposition is virtually impotent, and the government can enact whatever legislation it chooses, and carry into effect whatever policies it desires, in accordance with the ideology that inspires the single political party from which it has been formed. Readers must not only decide whether these merits of WTA are worth the sacrifice in the degree to which the electorate is represented in Parliament that WTA entails: they must decide whether they are merits at all. Because it seldom confers on any one party an absolute parliamentary majority, PR usually results in coalition governments. This leads to greater continuity of policy from election to election—usually a blessing, though sometimes a curse. Coalition governments are indeed often unstable: sometimes because the larger party has sought to bully its smaller partner, sometimes because the smaller one has sought to blackmail the larger, but also in response to swings in national opinion. Which consideration is the stronger is obviously a political question that readers must think out for themselves.

(9) In determining the right system for electing representatives, we have to choose between single-member constituencies and multi-member ones. This choice is usually
made with an eye to its effect on the composition of
Parliament. If the constituency principle is observed, single-
member constituencies tend to favour WW, and especially
so under the plurality system, while multi-member constituencies produce a national result approximating PR in its
standard form, because, under any reasonable electoral system, they will accord representation to minorities within the
constituency electorate, including minority parties. Even if
the dual-vote device is used, multi-member constituencies
will require fewer additional members if PR is aimed at,
while single-member constituencies will demand fewer if
the aim is WTA. If the dual-vote device is greatly disliked,
this will doubtless be the deciding factor in our choice
between them. If the dual-vote device is regarded as acceptable, on the other hand, the choice between single-member
and multi-member constituencies is better made by weigh-
ing their advantages in representing local electorates. Is it
better for an elector to have an MP who stands for a party
with which he may strongly disagree, but who represents a
small constituency with fairly homogeneous interests, or to
have one who sympathizes with his views and interests, and
is of a party he supports, even though he represents a large
area whose interests vary widely from one section of it to
another? This is eminently another political question for
readers to decide for themselves.

(10) There can be no electoral system that will never give
an advantage to tactical voters. Hence any recommendation
of a particular system that either states or insinuates that it

will give no such advantage should be disregarded: the propagandist is either ignorant or dishonest.

(11) The concept of the wasted vote is hopelessly confused, and, in many instances, impossible to apply. It should not be used as a basis for choosing an electoral system.

(12) When we consider what electoral system is best for selecting representatives of the constituencies, we must proceed, in accordance with principle (3), by first asking what criterion we should adopt for which candidate is, or which candidates are, the most representative, as shown by the electors' true preferences between them (supposing that we knew them). Having decided on this criterion, we should set about deciding how to get what we want by choosing, as the best electoral system, one that will always, or at least usually, result in the election of the most representative candidate or candidates, according to our criterion, provided that the electors all vote sincerely.

(13) If the electoral system in force generally produces a fair outcome, that is, the election, when all vote sincerely, of the most representative candidate or candidates, according to whatever criterion has been adopted for this, then, plainly, the occurrence of tactical voting will distort its operation. If it frequently fails to produce a fair outcome, then tactical voting will often make the outcome fairer than it would have been if all had voted sincerely. Tactical voting is nevertheless to be discouraged, because it gives an advantage to the well-informed irrelevant to the workings of democracy.

(14) Hence, before any electoral system is proposed, it must be scrutinized to see that it offers the least possible incentive to tactical voting. The most potent incentive to

vote tactically is provided by a system (such as the plurality system) that does not allow a voter to express all his preferences between the candidates. Any fair electoral system will therefore provide the means for each voter to rank all the candidates in order of preference.

(15) Evidently, the opportunity to rank all the candidates in order will have little effect in this regard if voters understand that certain of their preferences can never be taken into account. This creates a problem for anyone who believes that the right criterion for a candidate in a single-member constituency to be considered the most representative is that he should be the first choice of more voters than any other. This is the *only* such criterion that creates a virtually insoluble problem for anyone wishing to devise an electoral system that will, when all vote sincerely, result in the election of the candidate that satisfies the criterion, and yet will offer little incentive to vote tactically: just because a voter's preferences between candidates not of his first choice will be disregarded, the incentive will of necessity be extremely strong. Fortunately for the peace of mind of those considering the subject, the criterion is manifestly unsatisfactory. For both reasons, the plurality system is not a serious contender for a good method of electing one representative of a constituency.

(16) The two most plausible criteria for the most representative single candidate, in the light of voters' preferences, are those proposed by Condorcet and by Borda at the end of the eighteenth century. That of Condorcet is that a candidate is to be considered the most representative if, for each other candidate taken separately, he is preferred by a majority to that other candidate; he is the 'Condorcet

leader'. This criterion appeals to the strong intuitive conviction that, if a candidate is elected to whom a majority would have preferred some other, something inequitable is likely to have occurred. The criterion will convince all those imbued with what I called the 'mystique of the majority', that is to say, those who believe it to be intrinsic to democracy that in all circumstances the will of a majority should prevail.

(17) Borda's criterion, by contrast, treats every preference felt by any one voter for any candidate over another as of equal value. Moreover, it may be claimed for it that it takes better account of the strengths of preferences than does Condorcet's or any other based on majority preferences. It accords to a candidate standing three places higher than another in an elector's ranking 3 points more than the other, instead of merely taking account of the fact that the elector prefers him to the other: it treats relative position in the ranking as indicating strength of preference.

(18) Because Borda's criterion takes no particular account of majorities, it is better than Condorcet's at blocking highly contentious candidates, for it can block some of those who possess slender absolute majorities. The issue between Condorcet's and Borda's criteria turns on the importance to be attached to a majority. If there is just one proposal, to be accepted or rejected, then the wish of the majority must decide the matter; equally, when just one of two candidates is to be elected. But when a choice is to be made between three or more candidates, should we pay especial attention to a majority *as such*? If so, Condorcet was right; if not, then presumably Borda was.

(19) In this book, I have discussed the criteria of

Condorcet and Borda because I do not know, and have been unable to think of, any other that approaches either in plausibility. But in this matter as in others I am abjuring dogma. Any reader who knows, or can think of, one superior to both, must of course adopt it. The adoption of such a third criterion requires careful reflection, which should be informed by comparing the application of all three criteria to a variety of hypothetical cases.

(20) Condorcet's criterion is defective. Preferences may be so distributed that there is no Condorcet leader: whoever is elected, there will be another candidate whom a majority would have preferred. The criterion must therefore be supplemented, in such cases, by another. It may be supplemented directly by Borda's criterion: the most representative candidate should be taken to be the Condorcet leader, or, if there is none, the one having the highest Borda count. Or we may take account of the Copeland number of each candidate, namely the number of other candidates to whom he is preferred by a majority. In this case, the most representative candidate will be deemed to be that one, among those having Copeland numbers at least as high as those of any other candidates, who has the highest Borda count.

(21) These three criteria—the pure Borda count, the Condorcet criterion supplemented directly by the Borda count, and the Condorcet criterion supplemented first by the Copeland number criterion and then by the Borda count—correspond in an obvious way to electoral systems in which that candidate is elected who satisfies the relevant criterion, as calculated, not from the voters' actual preferences, but from those preferences as recorded on their ballot papers. These are the pure Borda system, the modified

comparison system, and the composite system. For single-member constituencies, the choice appears to be between these three, although the Borda system is arguably too vulnerable to tactical voting to be adopted. A reader who favours some other criterion for the most representative candidate will naturally have some other electoral system to propose.

(22) For multi-member constituencies, we need again first to decide on the right criterion for the candidates that ought to be elected. In this case, majorities are plainly irrelevant. The criterion that has here been proposed is that minorities of sufficient size, whether represented by a political party or not, should be accorded representation in Parliament; and that, if seats remain unfilled when this has been achieved, the most generally popular candidates deserve election. The feasible minimum size must depend on how many Members of Parliament the constituency is to return. To allow representation of the greatest number of minorities, if these reveal themselves by the pattern of voting, the quota used in STV is the right one: when there are five seats to be filled, a minority must form more than a sixth of the total number of voters, when only four seats, it must form more than a fifth, and so on. Borda scores (for individual candidates, not for overall outcomes) provide the only reasonable measure of the general popularity of a candidate. As before, I offer this dual criterion because it appears to me the only one worth consideration; the reader may decide to adopt some other.

(23) STV is the subject of intense, and not always very scrupulous, propaganda by many electoral reformers. Unless the subject is thought about by others who have hitherto

studied it very little, STV, without the dual-vote device, may well be adopted in Britain if electoral reform occurs there at all. For the first purpose stated under (22), the representation of minorities, STV is an ideal system. For the second purpose, the selection of the most generally popular candidates once the system has identified representatives of the minorities, it is all but hopeless. It is founded on no clear principle, and its operation is haphazard; very small variations in the votes cast can produce overwhelming changes in the final outcome. It has all the disadvantages of AV, and, since more candidates are involved, it has them in a higher degree.

(24) If the criterion of (22) is accepted, the solution is a system, here labelled QBS, that superimposes on the Borda system for individual candidates an overriding method of ensuring representation for minorities of sufficient size. The minorities are to be identified by the patterns of votes cast, namely by the existence of sufficiently extensive solid support for some set of candidates; the supporters rank all candidates in the set higher than any candidate not in it, although they do not all rank them in the same order. The representatives of the minorities thus identified are selected, not by a process of successive elimination, but by their Borda scores, with certain possible variations in the precise manner in which this is to be done.

Fervent believers in the plurality system will find much to criticize in this book. So will those for whom STV is an article of faith. I cannot see why anyone else should disagree with anything in it, especially since I have left so much for the reader to decide, without stating, and often without even hinting at, my own opinion. But I expect that there will be plenty of disagreement. I have not offered a solution to the problem of choosing an electoral system; I have tried only to clarify the questions that must be answered in order to find a solution. Some will dispute that I have succeeded even in doing that. I hope that they will at least concede that I have clarified them sufficiently to make it easy to see what mistakes I have made.

FURTHER READING

It is hard to compile a satisfactory bibliography in keeping with the spirit of this book, since most of the literature, if sound, is highly technical. The following somewhat random assortment contains books that will probably be found useful by readers. Those that will be especially useful to students are marked with an asterisk.

*Kenneth Arrow, *Social Choice and Individual Values* (New York, 1951; 2nd edn., 1963).

This short work effectively originated the study of social choice theory as an academic discipline. It is expressed in a technical manner, but requires virtually no prior knowledge.

*Duncan Black, *The Theory of Committees and Elections* (Cambridge, 1958).

This book is by a pioneer in the subject among modern writers; though not up to date, it is fairly easy to understand. The appendix, reprinting pamphlets by C. L. Dodgson (Lewis Carroll), will be found to be clear and illuminating.

Steven J. Brams and Peter C. Fishburn, *Approval Voting* (Boston, 1983).

This little book, by two experts in social choice theory, advocates an electoral system of their devising, not discussed in the present book, which readers may find attractive.

*Michael Dummett, *Voting Procedures* (Oxford, 1984).

The literature on the mathematical theory of voting is enormous. This was an attempt to convey to people practically concerned with voting methods those of its results of immediate relevance to them; it is much more technical than the present book, and deals specifically with electoral systems only in the last two chapters. There is an extensive bibliography.

Peter Emerson, *The Politics of Consensus* (Belfast, 1994).

This is a stimulating little book by an enthusiast for Borda-type systems.

*Robin Farquharson, *The Theory of Voting* (New Haven, Conn., 1969).

This short book, written eleven years before it was published, expounded a highly original approach to a subject that barely existed when it was written. It is very easy to understand, although it uses some technical vocabulary.

Arend Lijphart and Bernard Grofman (eds.), *Choosing an Electoral System: Issues and Alternatives* (New York, 1984).

This is a volume of essays by different hands and very diverse opinions. Some of the essays are very useful.

Iain McLean, *Public Choice: An Introduction* (Oxford, 1987).

Only one chapter of this book deals with the theory of electoral systems, but it is a good introduction to the general background of the subject.

Robert A. Newland, *Comparative Electoral Systems* (London, 1982; distributed by the Electoral Reform Society).

This is a short booklet giving basic information about electoral methods. The author's opinions are not always reliable, though he is less partisan than most Electoral Reform Society writers; but the information is lucidly and succinctly conveyed.

*Amartya Sen, *Collective Choice and Social Welfare* (San Francisco and Amsterdam, 1970).

*Amartya Sen, *Choice, Welfare, and Measurement* (Oxford, 1982).

These two books are by a celebrated economist who is a master of social choice theory; the second is a collection of essays of great general interest.

Leslie Sykes, *Proportional Representation: Which System?* (Leicester, 1990).

This little booklet criticizes STV, and strongly advocates the German system (which was the West German system when it was written).

INDEX